100 Prized Poems
Twenty-five years of the Forward Books
Edited by William Sieghart

This anthology was designed and produced by Bookmark, sponsor of the Prizes. Bookmark is a global content and communications company based in London, Toronto, Montreal, Santiago, Lima, New York, LA, Shanghai and Singapore. Bookmark uses consumer insights to develop measurable marketing strategies and creative propositions to engage consumers, drive sales, and transform brands. Clients include Patek Philippe, Air Canada, LATAM, Bombardier, Fairmont Hotels & Resorts, Explora, Standard Life, Tesco, American Express Travel, Mercedes-Benz, Christie's, Lindt, the Academy of St Martin in the Fields and StreetSmart. bookmarkcontent.com @bookmarkcontent

100 Prized Poems
Twenty-five years of the
Forward Books

Edited by William Sieghart

BOOKMARK

LONDON

First published in Great Britain by
Forward Worldwide · 83 Clerkenwell Road · London EC1R 5AR
in association with
Faber & Faber · Bloomsbury House · 74-77 Great Russell Street
London WC1B 3DA
2 4 6 8 10 9 7 5 3 1

ISBN 978 0 571 33317 2 (paperback)

Compilation copyright © Bookmark 2016
Cover image and design copyright © Sophie Herxheimer

Printed and bound by CPI Group (UK) Ltd, Croydon CR0 4YY

A CIP catalogue reference for this book
is available at the British Library.

To Susannah Herbert

Contents

Preface by William Sieghart, founder of the Forward Prizes for Poetry   xi

Moniza Alvi · The Sari   3

Simon Armitage · Poundland   4

Mona Arshi · What Every Girl Should Know Before Marriage   6

Ros Barber · Material   8

George Barker · On a Bird Dead in the Road   11

Fiona Benson · Breastfeeding   12

Judi Benson · Burying the Ancestors   14

Emily Berry · Letter to Husband   19

Liz Berry · Nailmaking   20

Kate Bingham · Monogamy   21

Eavan Boland · Inheritance   23

Pat Boran · Waving   24

Kamau Brathwaite · *from* Agoue   26

Colette Bryce · Derry   29

John Burnside · History   33

Matthew Caley · Eight Ways Of Looking At Lakes   36

Vahni Capildeo · Stalker   39

Anne Carson · God's Justice   40

Ciaran Carson · Alibi   41

Kate Clanchy · War Poetry   43

Gillian Clarke · Anorexic   44

Wendy Cope · Two Cures for Love   46

Robert Crawford · Ferrari   47

Allan Crosbie · Manifesto   48

Kwame Dawes · New Neighbours   50

Imtiaz Dharker · Its face   51

Michael Donaghy · My Flu   52

Tishani Doshi · Turning into Men Again   53

Jane Draycott · No. 3 *from* Uses for the Thames 54

Carol Ann Duffy · Valentine 55

Ian Duhig · The Lammas Hireling 56

Helen Dunmore · To my nine-year-old self 57

UA Fanthorpe · Atlas 59

Paul Farley · Liverpool Disappears for a Billionth of a Second 60

Vicki Feaver · Judith 61

Duncan Forbes · Recension Day 62

Linda France · Cooking with Blood 63

Matthew Francis · The Ornamental Hermit 64

Pamela Gillilan · Three Ways to a Silk Shirt 66

Alan Gillis · Bulletin from The Daily Mail 68

John Goodby · The Uncles 69

Lavinia Greenlaw · A World Where News Travelled Slowly 70

Thom Gunn · Lament 71

Jen Hadfield · Definitions 75

Tony Harrison · A Cold Coming 79

David Harsent · The Curator 87

Seamus Heaney · The Blackbird of Glanmore 89

Stuart Henson · The Price 91

WN Herbert · Smirr 92

Geoffrey Hill · *from* The Orchards of Syon 93

Selima Hill · Please Can I Have a Man 94

Ellen Hinsey · XVII Correspondences: Aphorisms Regarding Impatience 95

Sarah Howe · Tame 97

Ted Hughes · Flounders 99

Clive James · Holding Court 101

Kathleen Jamie · Speirin 103

Alan Jenkins · Effects 104

Linton Kwesi Johnson · Mi Revalueshanary Fren 106

Jackie Kay · Late Love 110

Mimi Khalvati · The Swarm 111

John Kinsella · The Hierarchy of Sheep – a report from my brother   112

August Kleinzahler · Epistle XXXIX   115

RF Langley · To a Nightingale   116

James Lasdun · Stones   118

Gwyneth Lewis · Mother Tongue   120

Michael Longley · Cloudberries   122

Hannah Lowe · Dance Class   123

Roddy Lumsden · Yeah Yeah Yeah   124

Derek Mahon · Death in Bangor   125

Glyn Maxwell · The Byelaws   128

Roger McGough · The Way Things Are   129

Jamie McKendrick · Home Thoughts   131

Kei Miller · in which the cartographer asks for directions   132

Sinéad Morrissey · The Coal Jetty   133

Paul Muldoon · Wire   136

Les Murray · The Shield-Scales of Heraldry   138

Daljit Nagra · Look We Have Coming to Dover!   140

Sean O'Brien · The Politics of   141

Alice Oswald · A Greyhound in the Evening after a Long Day of Rain   142

Don Paterson · Nil Nil   144

Clare Pollard · Thinking of England   147

Peter Porter · Last Words   152

Sheenagh Pugh · Envying Owen Beattie   153

Claudia Rankine · The new therapist specializes…   155

Denise Riley · Listening for lost people   156

Michael Symmons Roberts · Pika   157

Robin Robertson · At Roane Head   158

Jacob Sam-La Rose · After Lazerdrome, McDonalds, Peckham Rye   160

Ann Sansom · Voice   162

Carole Satyamurti · Striking Distance   163

Jo Shapcott · Vegetable Love   165

Owen Sheers · Old Horse, New Tricks   167

Penelope Shuttle · Outgrown   168

George Szirtes · Actually, yes   169

Kate Tempest · Thirteen   170

RS Thomas · Geriatric   171

Derek Walcott · White Egrets   172

Lucy Anne Watt · The Tree Position   173

Hugo Williams · Joy   175

Benjamin Zephaniah · Man to Man   176

Biographies   179

Publisher acknowledgements   199

Winners of the Forward Prizes   205

Preface

This anthology – 100 poems by 100 poets – is a distillation of the 25 annual Forward books of poetry published since 1992. In that year George Bush and Boris Yeltsin declared the Cold War officially over. The first McDonald's opened in China. Diana, Princess of Wales, separated from her husband. The Maastricht treaty created the European Union. The end of the world, predicted by a Korean Christian cult for 28 October, did not occur.

In that month, a jury chaired by Stephen Spender awarded the first Forward Prizes for Poetry: Thom Gunn won the Best Collection prize for *The Man with Night Sweats*, while Simon Armitage, a probation officer from Manchester, collected the cheque for Most Promising Young Poet, and Jackie Kay walked off with the Best Single Poem award.

As the prizes' founder, I enjoyed the buzz, the applause for the poets, the headlines – but most of all, I relished seeing the first *Forward Book of Poetry* take shape. This anthology, which brought together poems by the shortlisted and commended writers, would, I hoped, inspire readers to discover the excitement of new poetry.

I wanted others, possibly years from then, to be as delighted by it as I had been on finding a second-hand copy of a 1959 *Guinness Book of Poetry*, in which WH Auden's 'Goodbye to the Mezzogiorno' and Robert Lowell's 'Skunk Hour' figured alongside works by the likes of Ted Hughes, Elizabeth Jennings, Thom Gunn and Philip Larkin. Memorably, Larkin's masterpiece 'The Whitsun Weddings' was in the book's Other Poems section after failing to make the judges' final cut for that year's Guinness Prize.

I had, in 1992, no idea that the Forwards would develop into a series, but as a young publisher – ignorant of the coming seductions of mobile phones and social media – I was convinced that the book mattered. Headlines are all very well, but there is something invidious about giving prizes to three poets if the others are cast into lasting shadow. In an anthology, all have a share in the light.

There are several poets in that first Forward book who were not called to accept a prize at the time, but who are now recognised as among the greats of our age: Alice Keen, known now as Alice Oswald, is one. I've chosen 'A Greyhound in the Evening after a Long Day of Rain' to represent her here, rather than the far longer work, 'Dunt', for which she later won the Best Single Poem award. From the same year, I chose works by Linton Kwesi Johnson, and Tony Harrison – whose shockingly prescient 'A Cold Coming' gives voice to a corpse in the first Iraq war.

If such important names look strange, strung together among the also-rans for that first year, then stranger still is my sense, on re-reading more than 1,600 poems featured in all the Forward books to date, that I'm no closer to knowing what constitutes a 'stayer', a poem that will last. All I can say, echoing many of the hundred-odd judges, is that you learn to suspect any poem that goes down too easily, leaving no trace in the memory. Good poems grow in the re-reading: anthologists and juries, like expert gardeners, know something of the material they are dealing with, but they cannot know what future eyes will see.

This uncertainty means that the word 'best' – used to promote the books and prizes each year – is always provisional. I take consolation from TS Eliot's use of the term. 'The best contemporary poetry,' he wrote in 1942, 'can give us a feeling of excitement and a sense of fulfilment different from any sentiment aroused even by very much greater poetry of a past age.'

Inevitably my own quest for that 'feeling of excitement' and 'sense of fulfilment' has determined my choices, but I have also sought poems that will connect with the widest possible range of readers. Back in the 1990s, the UK and Ireland were different: it was, for example, entirely unexceptional for authoritative anthologies of twentieth-century poetry to contain four times as many men as women, all, or almost all, white. The contemporary canon as monolith belongs to history now: and a close study of the Forward books over the years shows how change can happen. The 2016 chair of judges, Malika Booker, pinpoints Kwame Dawes' selection as the winner of the Best First Collection prize in 1994 as her own Eureka moment, inspiring her to create a writing community for poets outside the monolith. Programmes like the Arts Council's Complete Works have transformed poetry publishing by offering support to writers who lacked the networks that eased the path to publication in the past. I am glad that the Forwards have played – and continue to play – a modest part in this process.

Some contributors to this book won a Forward Prize more than once – Sean O'Brien, Don Paterson, Robin Robertson – but in the interest of pace, I have chosen just one poem to represent each poet. Some writers who featured in two earlier compilation volumes (the *Poems of the Decade* books) have been omitted, so that buyers of all three compilations do not feel short-changed. I was guided by the need to include poems long and short, to provoke thought, wonder and every shade of emotion.

When I doubt, I have asked myself if anyone in 10 or 20 years' time, opening this book, would find it rewarding. More than 6,000 teenagers are currently studying for English Literature A Level with the Edexcel board: their exams will include questions on the most recent *Poems of the Decade* book, which has been chosen as a set text. This is the highest compliment anyone could pay to the work of the poets, publishers and judges who have shaped the Forward 'canon'. Those hours spent reading, arguing, revising and selecting have not been wasted. I wish no less for this collection. It is commonplace to speak of anthologies as bunches of flowers: this one is a bag of seeds. I hope some fall on fertile ground.

Thanks to all who have been involved in the making of this book, particularly Bookmark, previously Forward Worldwide, whose team of editors and designers has, for 25 years, repeatedly dedicated time, skill and generosity to bringing out the book. As sponsors of both the prizes and the books since the start, Bookmark has been exemplary: we are very lucky. The following know how much we owe them: Will Scott, Casey Jones, Christopher Stocks, Simon Hobbs, Lucy Coles, Gordon Hodge, Ian Batts and Chris Carus. Ed Victor, Dotti Irving and Liz Sich were the midwives to the venture and ensured its high profile for the first two decades. Joanna Mackle, then of Faber, gave us her enthusiastic backing on day one and is still a valued trustee of the Forward Arts Foundation.

In more recent years, Rebecca Blackwood and Clare Cumberlidge of Thirteen Ways enabled us to grow. Forward Arts Foundation has been transformed by Susannah Herbert and Maisie Lawrence in the past four years: they know how grateful I am. They persuaded Sophie Herxheimer, artist and poet, to create this book's stunning cover.

And finally, of course, thanks to the Forward alumni – all the poets and judges. We list them, with thanks, on our website forwardartsfoundation.org.

William Sieghart, *July 2016*

100 Prized Poems
Twenty-five years of the Forward Books

Moniza Alvi

The Sari

Inside my mother
I peered through a glass porthole.
The world beyond was hot and brown.

They were all looking in on me –
Father, Grandmother,
the cook's boy, the sweeper-girl,
the bullock with the sharp
shoulderblades,
the local politicians.

My English grandmother
took a telescope
and gazed across continents.

All the people unravelled a sari.
It stretched from Lahore to Hyderabad,
wavered across the Arabian Sea,
shot through with stars,
fluttering with sparrows and quails.
They threaded it with roads,
undulations of land.

Eventually
they wrapped and wrapped me in it
whispering *Your body is your country*.

Simon Armitage

Poundland

Came we then to the place abovementioned,
crossed its bristled threshold through robotic glass doors,
entered its furry heat, its flesh-toned fluorescent light.
Thus with wire-wrought baskets we voyaged,
and some with trolleys, back wheels flipping like trout tails,
cruised the narrow canyons twixt cascading shelves,
the prow of our journeying cleaving stale air.
Legion were the items that came tamely to hand:
five stainless steel teaspoons, ten corn-relief plasters,
the busy bear pedal bin liners fragranced with country lavender,
the Disney design calendar and diary set, three cans of Vimto,
cornucopia of potato-based snacks and balm for a sweet tooth,
toys and games, goods of Orient made, and of Cathay,
all under the clouded eye of CCTV,
beyond the hazard cone where serious chutney spillage had occurred.
Then emerged souls: the duty manager with a face like Doncaster,
mumbling, 'For so much, what shall we give in return?'
The blood-stained employee of the month,
sobbing on a woolsack of fun-fur rugs,
many uniformed servers, spectral, drifting between aisles.
Then came Elpenor, our old friend Elpenor,
slumped and shrunken by the Seasonal Products display.
In strangled words I managed,
'How art thou come to these shady channels, into hell's ravine?'
And he: '*To loan sharks I owe/the bone and marrow of my all.*'
Then Walt Whitman, enquiring politely of the delivery boy.
And from Special Occasions came forth Tiresias,
dead in life, alive in death, cider-scented and sock-less,
Oxfam-clad, shaving cuts to both cheeks, quoting the stock exchange.
And my own mother reaching out, slipping a tin of stewing steak
to the skirt pocket of her wedding dress,
blessed with a magician's touch, practised in need.

But never until the valley widened at the gated brink
did we open our lips to fish out those corn-coloured coins,
those minted obols, hard won tokens graced with our monarch's head,
kept hidden beneath the tongue's eel, blood-tasting,
both ornament and safeguard, of armour made.
And paid forthwith, then broke surface
and breathed extraordinary daylight into starved lungs,
steered for home through precincts and parks scalded by polar winds,
laden with whatnot, lightened of golden quids.

Mona Arshi

What Every Girl Should Know Before Marriage

after Sujata Bhatt

Eliminating thought verbs is the key to a successful marriage.

You're better off avoiding the reach for specificity and
curbing your interest in the interior of things.

The cobra always reverts to TYPE, tuneless
girls tend to wither on the vine.

Oil of jasmine will arouse river fish.

In the poetry of the Sung Dynasty the howling of monkeys
in gorges was used to express profound desolation.

Things you should have a good working knowledge
of: mitochondria, Roman roads, field glasses, making
rice (using the evaporation method only).

When your mother in law calls you smart,
it's not meant as a compliment.

The lighter her eyes, the further she'll travel.

Always have saffron in your kitchen cupboard
(but on no account ever use it).

*Taunt the sky during the day; the stars
will be your hazard at night.*

Do not underestimate the art of small talk. Learn some stock phrases such as 'they say Proust was an insufferable hypochondriac' or 'I'm confident that the Government will discharge their humanitarian obligations.'

Fasting sharpens the mind and is therefore
a good time to practise reverse flight.

Your husband may not know you cheated with shop-bought *garam masala* but God will know.

Ros Barber

Material

My mother was the hanky queen
when hanky meant a thing of cloth,
not paper tissues bought in packs
from late-night garages and shops,
but things for waving out of trains
and mopping the corners of your grief:
when hankies were material
she'd have one, always, up her sleeve.

Tucked in the wrist of every cardi,
a mum's embarrassment of lace
embroidered with a V for Viv,
spittled and scrubbed against my face.
And sometimes more than one fell out
as if she had a farm up there
where dried-up hankies fell in love
and mated, raising little squares.

She bought her own; I never did.
Hankies were presents from distant aunts
in boxed sets, with transparent covers
and script initials spelling *ponce*,
the naffest Christmas gift you'd get –
my brothers too, more often than not,
got male ones: serious, and grey,
and larger, like they had more snot.

It was hankies that closed department stores,
with headscarves, girdles, knitting wool
and trouser presses; homely props
you'd never find today in malls.
Hankies, which demanded irons,

and boiling to be purified
shuttered the doors of family stores
when those who used to buy them died.

And somehow, with the hanky's loss,
greengrocer George with his dodgy foot
delivering veg from a Comma van
is history, and the friendly butcher
who'd slip an extra sausage in,
the fishmonger whose marble slab
of haddock smoked the colour of yolks
and parcelled rows of local crab

lay opposite the dancing school
where Mrs White, with painted talons,
taught us *When You're Smiling* from
a stumbling, out of tune piano:
step-together, step-together, step-together,
point! The Annual Talent Show
when every mother, fencing tears,
would whip a hanky from their sleeve
and smudge the rouge from little dears.

Nostalgia only makes me old.
The innocence I want my brood
to cling on to like ten-bob notes
was killed in TV's lassitude.
And it was me that turned it on
to buy some time to write this poem
and eat bought biscuits I would bake
if I'd commit to being home.

There's never a hanky up my sleeve.
I raised neglected-looking kids,
the kind whose noses strangers clean.
What awkwardness in me forbids

me to keep tissues in my bag
when handy packs are 50p?
I miss material handkerchiefs,
their soft and hidden history.

But it isn't mine. I'll let it go.
My mother too, eventually,
who died not leaving handkerchiefs
but tissues and uncertainty:
and she would say, should I complain
of the scratchy and disposable,
that *this is your material*
to do with, daughter, what you will.

George Barker

On a Bird Dead in the Road

What formerly flounced and flew its fantastic feathers
Now lies like a flattened old leather glove in the road,
And the gigantic wheels of the articulated juggernaut lorries
Pound down on it all day long like the mad will of god.

Fiona Benson

Breastfeeding

i

But really it's like this –
weeping as your milk comes in,
clutching a hot poultice
and counting through the pain
as you bring her on
to the hardened breast.

There's a whole new grammar
of tongue-tie and latch –
the watery foremilk
with its high acid content,
the fatty hindmilk
that separates in the fridge

to a thick skim
at the top of the flask,
and the nursing bra
like a complex lock
as you fumble, one-handed
at the catch.

ii

She has a stomach
the size of a marble
and feeds in and out
of days.

You are lost
to the manifold
stations of milk,
the breast siphoned off

then filling,
yellow curd
of the baby's shit
you get down on your knees

at the foot of the change-mat
to clean,
holding your breath.
It was always like this;

a long line of women
sitting and kneeling,
out of their skins
with love and exhaustion.

Judi Benson

Burying the Ancestors

I

I'm tired of being crooned to the tune
of old Aunt Liza's dead goose,
lullabyed in those cotton fields back home,
roused to Dixie, swamped in the Sewanee River,
hearing Mammy say *hush chile*,
you know your Mamma was born to die.
The one they called Morning, born into the light,
taking her mamma's life. *Hush chile. Hush Mammy*.

I want the repeat names to stop repeating,
all those Henry fathers, greats and grands,
uncles, brothers, cousins intertwined, intermarried.
Juniors, Seniors, and all those Roman numerals, just delete.

Set fire to the tissue-thin letters of fine penmanship
and not much to say, *weather's fine*,
coming home in the covered wagon.
Clip the stamps, give them to the collector,
then burn baby burn.

Burn all their blusterings, their justifications
for blistering others' skin in the relentless summer heat,
while they wrapped themselves around shady porches.

I know to honour this blood flowing through me
is to say nothing. Don't mention the wills
begetting slaves and all their increase, forever, amen.
Sadie, Cicely, Moses, Caesar, and the one they called Patience.
Chains around their necks, chains around their ankles,
chains around their hopeless hearts,
all for the increase of those who refused to work the land,
whose hands were forbidden to touch dirt.

But my tongue wants to be released from its stays.
All those big hats bouncing with flowers, tossed in the wind,
pale faces unveiled, finding a trace of the darker hue hinted at.

II

Let Eugenia in her ball gown go waltzing
back out the door. Stop fanning her lashes at the Judge,
begging him to pass the Secession Act on her birthday.
Pretty please Judge, I'll be 19. And so he did,
slicing Georgia off from the Union.

And then what, and what if only Johnny
had come marching home again.
Eugenia, dead of night, bundling her babies
into the flat wagon, crossing the rising river,
just before the bridge gave out,
whipping the horses and cursing those damn Yankees
she'd never forgive, nor all her increase.

Eugenia always seen in mourning-black,
burying her father, her babies, her husband.
Rocking on her porch, silver-haired,
a black ribbon round her neck, glint in her eye,
sure the South would rise again.

III

Soft people, hard people, lines crissing and crossing
the economic divide, rattling at the edges of china cups,
hands cracked from hard work, soft hands slipping into gloves.
Ladies and Gents, rebels and ruffians.

These strangers: Benjamin, Lydia, Josh and Jasmine,
flattened in the black and white photograph,
sitting stiffly, even when casual,
suspicious of the man under black cloth
the little box with the sudden *Pop!*
Smile? Say cheese? What's that.

Meat? No one's had any in months,
cracked corn, bucked wheat,
and always hoe cake, though once
it was told, syrup.

Once the land was fertile.
Then grew to be like its people, over-worked, exhausted,
tobacco, cotton, corn, thirsty for rain.
The great greats and not-so-greats
with their sharp pulled-back hair,
tight knots, tributaries of trouble
running across their faces,
bending their mouths down,
bones edging through the little skin.
Even the old-eyed children
clench an angry desperation in their faces.

Left-overs, that was all some could afford to rent.
All they had, they'd inherited, the feather bed,
one scrawny mule, three slaves and all their increase.
Just another mouth to feed.

IV
Planters, plantation owners, preachers, politicians,
doctors, lawyers, artists, teachers, n'er do wells, drunks,
do-gooders, glamour girls posing for Coca Cola ads:
Camille, Vally, Lamar,
naughty girls seen smoking in public, racey women,
swell men, bootleg whisky, speakeasys, suicides,
insanity, vanity and humility. Anecdotes and ancient history,
all it boils down to. Stories told, changed in the telling.

Henry was driving through the back roads in his Model T,
so fast he killed a bunch of chickens on the dusty Georgia clay.
'Hey Mister, you gotta pay,' shouts the irate farmer.
'How much?' 'Make it fifteen bucks.'
'Here's 30 cause I'm comin back just as fast.'

Little Henry, Big Henry, dead Henry.

Some lost to sea, some to land. War heroes,
influenza victims, gamblers, ladies' men,
loose women, tight-laced Baptists, Huguenots,
shouting Methodists,
Klan members and Abolitionists,
Suffragettes and Southern Belles,
side by side now, bones mouldering together,
mixing up the arguments, leaving all that love hanging.

v

They were just people, sugah, father said,
*they worked hard and were honest. Religious folk,
never played cards on Sunday, never mixed with coloreds.*
Amen. Praise the Lord and pass the ammunition,
pass the succotash, pass the buck, cross yourself,
swear to tell the truth, pray the Lord your soul to take
and all that hate: Absalom, Walter, Kitty, Caroline,
Dolly with the hole in her stocking, dance with her,
dance with all her dead. Jason with the hole in his head, fix it.
The named and never named, the never talked about one
who ran away with the chauffeur, the older one who stayed,
the one forever missing in action,
the ones whose minds flew away.

VI

Go away then, I tell them. Stop your whispering in shadows,
plucking at my scalp, sucking at my conscience.
Half-words almost heard,
how my hands are too soft and my thinking too,
how we've all gone soft.

They puzzle over the flushing of the loo.
Wonder why we waste the rich soil
they gave their lives to,
growing flowers that bear no fruit.

Lena, Ezekiel, Liza, Jebediah.
Names without faces, faces without names.

Go back to Georgia, Kentucky, Tennessee, Maryland,
Virginia, up on over the border to Pennsylvania.
Go back over to the side you should have fought on.
Change the colour of your uniform,
change your vote, change the fate, un-buy those slaves,
uncrack the cowhide, unlick your lips, that hunger
you have for black skin to lash, your tongue a weapon,
quoting the Good Book, washing your hands clean in holy water.

Leave the land to the Natives who know how to honour it.
Get back on that ship to England,
cross the channel back to France.
Take the Master out of Mister. Take off the H
you added to the family name. Return to your mother-tongue,
parlez vous again in the city you came from,
before they chased you out, or the grass got greener,
before the drought, the flood,
before some great great named John
went down with the ship called Increase,
before the long bitter of it all got passed down,
before the going down to the frozen ground
of the one without a name.

Call her Peace and let her rest. Amen.

Emily Berry

Letter to Husband

Dearest husband   Beloved husband   Most respected,
missed and righteous husband   Dear treasured, absent
husband   Dear unimaginable piece of husband
Dear husband of the moon,   it has been six months since I
Dear much lamented distant husband, my champing   heart
forgives you   please come.   In a long
undergrowth of wanting I creep   at night the sea is a dark room
I called and called   These white corridors are not
free from longing   Dear postman   Dear night-time, dear
dark mouth hovering over me   Dear knee bones
dear palms, dear faithful   body   I have wants

Husband –   Speech is a dark stain spreading
I have no telephone   No one will give me a telephone
I lost your voice   in dark places   it is written
over and over   that   please come.
A scribble is the way a heartbeat is told   Dearest serrated
husband. My heartscribbles   your name. My mouth
scribbles: I have cried your name in every
possible colour I have given you my proud   desperate
undeviating wish   over and over and over: Sweetheart, please come

Liz Berry

Nailmaking

Nailing was wenches' werk.
Give a girl of eight an anvil and a little ommer
and by God er'd swing it,
batter the glowing iron into tidy spikes
ready fer hoofing some great sod oss
who'd lost its shoe in the muck.

The nimble ones was best,
grew sharp and quick as the nails they struck
from the scorching fire.
Eighteen, er could turn out two hundred an hour,
tongue skimming the soot on er lips,
onds moulding heat.

In the small brick nailshop
four of 'em werked wi' faces glistening
in the hot smoke. Fust the point was forged
then the rod sunk deep into the bore
so the head could be punched –
round fer regulars, diamond fer frost nails.

Marry a nailing fella and yo'll be a pit oss
fer life, er sisters had told er,
but er'd gone to him anyway in er last white frock
and found a new black ommer
waiting fer er in 'is nailshop
under a tablecloth veil.

ommer hammer; *er* her, she; *oss* horse

Kate Bingham

Monogamy

I blame it on the backlash: free love
in the Eighties was for hippies, no one
liked Thatcher but monogamy
seemed more efficient, comforting to State
and individual alike, less last
resort than a celebration in bed

of the right to choose, not make your bed
and lie in it so much as a labour of love
we willingly fell in with, certain at last:
I wanted you, you wanted me. Alone
for the first time and in no fit state
for company we didn't see monogamy –

dumb, satisfied, unsung monogamy –
sneak in and slide between us on the bed,
backdating itself as if to reinstate
respectability, disguised as love's
romantic ideal and mocking our offhand, one
night stand bravado. It wants us to last,

our happiness, like a disease, its last
chance to spread – as if monogamy
transmits non-sexually from one
adoring couple to the next – to embed
itself in a world where pleasure and love
live separately and sit again in state,

pass sentence on what neither Church nor State
condemn outright. But what if we do last?
Time's not the test. Who loves best won't always love
longest, might not respect monogamy's
insistence, its assumption that all beds
must be forsaken but the one

one lies in in love. My eyes are for no one
but you, my love. We lie in a state
of easy innocence, a bed
of roses, tumbled and fragrant to the last
linen bud, but what's monogamy
without temptation, faith without love?

Therefore for love we should sacrifice one
thing alone: monogamy; maintain a state
of mutual jealousy, outlast our bed.

Eavan Boland

Inheritance

I have been wondering
what I have to leave behind, to give my daughters.

No good offering the view
between here and Three Rock Mountain,
the blueness in the hours before rain, the long haze afterwards.
The ground I stood on was never really mine. It might not ever
    be theirs.

And gifts that were passed through generations –
silver and the fluid light left after silk – were never given here.

This is an island of waters, inland distances,
with a history of want and women who struggled
to make the nothing which was all they had
into something they could leave behind.

I learned so little from them: the lace bobbin with its braided mesh,
its oat-straw pillow and the wheat-coloured shawl
knitted in one season
to imitate another

are all crafts I never had
and can never hand on. But then again there was a night
I stayed awake, alert and afraid, with my first child
who turned and turned; sick, fretful.

When dawn came I held my hand over the absence of fever,
over skin which had stopped burning, as if I knew the secrets
of health and air, as if I understood them

and listened to the silence
and thought, I must have learned that somewhere.

Pat Boran

Waving

As a child I waved to people I didn't know.
I waved from passing cars, school buses,
second-floor windows, or from the street
to secretaries trapped in offices above.
When policemen motioned my father on
past the scene of the crime or an army checkpoint,
I waved back from the back seat. I loved to wave.
I saw the world disappear into a funnel
of perspective, like the reflection in a bath
sucked into a single point when the water
drains. I waved in greeting at things that vanished
into points. I waved to say, 'I see you: can you see me?'

I loved 'the notion of an ocean' that could wave,
of a sea that rose up to see the onlooker
standing on the beach. And though the sea
came towards the beach, it was a different sea
when it arrived; the onlooker too had changed.
They disappeared, both of them, into points in time.
So that was why they waved to one another.
On the beach I waved until my arms hurt.

My mother waved her hair sometimes. This,
I know, seems to be something else. But,
when she came up the street, bright and radiant,
her white hair like a jewel-cap on her head,
it was a signal I could not fail to answer.
I waved and she approached me, smiling shyly.

Sometimes someone walking beside her
might wave back, wondering where they knew me from.
Hands itched in pockets, muscles twitched
when I waved. 'There's someone who sees me!'

But in general people took no risk with strangers.
And when they saw who I was – or wasn't –
they felt relief, saved from terrible disgrace.

Now it turns out that light itself's a wave
(as well as a point, or points), so though the waving's
done, it's really only just beginning. Whole humans –
arms, legs, backs, bellies – are waving away,
flickering on and off, in and out of time
and space, pushing through streets with heads down,
smiling up at office windows, lying in gutters
with their kneecaps broken and their hopes dashed,
driving, loving, hiding, growing old, and always
waving, waving as if to say: 'Can you see me?
I can see you – still…still…still…'

Kamau Brathwaite

from **Agoue**

a sequence for
VOICE . CHORAL CHORUS . MUSIC
& VODOUNISTAS
*the music is im brooks . the vision is temne callender . the painting
gérard valsin*

*

first there is this frost and it was light

blue almost white
like cloud. icing of furushima
and then it was real cloud. like the blue

mountains

and then there are two loaves
of land. brown. w/ straight
lines in them. running up out of the dark

water

and these loaves are a distant island
like humps of a brontosaurus. w/out its head
or tail. sailing into the true

water

and the water is serene like peace and make a straight
line like anguilla
like ink under that scaly island

and there is the faintest breath of wind
upon these waters
so that it make no waves

only a gentile heave
or heaven where there would be fry
or shrimp or louvres

.

and then the fish

jump
-silver . w/ red torch-
light eyes . the fins shining like steel terraces

or lovers

out of the palm trees green

and then the seven
-brothers of the rain-
bow . also

fish

jump straight up . in the air

two

from the one

three

one

-from the x-
act other

and in the royal centre
of the purple
tuning now softly to light

-in-
digo blue
dissolve of the darkness of blue

are the four

-w/ leopard stops and scissor-
-tails all-
-most in air. all-

most in water
brothers flying from branches to irie
. and as they fly .

whale & sirène

. not flying . not falling .
but like flow
-ing-
-flow-
-ing-
-flow-
-ing-

Colette Bryce

Derry

I was born between the Creggan and the Bogside
    to the sounds of crowds and smashing glass,
by the river Foyle with its suicides and rip tides.
    I thought that city was nothing less

than the whole and rain-domed universe.
    A teacher's daughter, I was one of nine
faces afloat in the looking-glass
    fixed in the hall, but which was mine?

I wasn't ever sure.
    We walked to school, linked hand in hand
in twos and threes like paper dolls.
    I slowly grew to understand

the way the grey Cathedral cast
    its shadow on our learning, cool,
as sunlight crept from east to west.
    The adult world had tumbled into hell

from where it wouldn't find its way
    for thirty years. The local priest
played Elvis tunes and made us pray
    for starving children, and for peace,

and lastly for 'The King'. At mass we'd chant
    hypnotically, *Hail Holy Queen*,
mother of mercy; sing to Saint
    Columba of his *Small oak grove, O Derry mine.*

*

We'd cross the border in our red Cortina,
    stopped at the checkpoint just too long
for fractious children, searched by a teenager
    drowned in a uniform, cumbered with a gun,

who seemed to think we were trouble-on-the-run
    and not the Von Trapp Family Singers
harmonizing every song
    in rounds to pass the journey quicker.

Smoke coiled up from terraces
    and fog meandered softly down the valley
to the Brandywell and the greyhound races,
    the ancient walls with their huge graffiti,

arms that encircled the old city
    solidly. Beyond their pale,
the Rossville flats – mad vision of modernity;
    snarling crossbreeds leashed to rails.

A robot under remote control like us
    commenced its slow acceleration
towards a device at number six,
    home of the moderate politician;

only a hoax, for once, some boys
    had made from parcel tape and batteries
gathered on forays to the BSR,
    the disused electronics factory.

                    *

The year was nineteen eighty-one,
    the reign of Thatcher. 'Under Pressure'
was the song that played from pub to pub
    where talk was all of hunger strikers

in the Maze, our jail within a jail.
    A billboard near Free Derry Corner
clocked the days to the funerals
    as riots blazed in the city centre.

Each day, we left for the grammar school,
    behaved ourselves, pulled up our socks
for benevolent Sister Emmanuel
    and the Order of Mercy. Then we'd flock

to the fleet of buses that ferried us
    back to our lives, the Guildhall Square
where Shena Burns our scapegoat drunk
    swayed in her chains like a dancing bear.

On the couch, we cheered as an Irish man
    bid for the Worldwide Featherweight title
and I saw blue bruises on my mother's arms
    when her sleeve fell back while filling the kettle

for tea. My bed against the door,
    I pushed the music up as loud
as it would go and curled up on the floor
    to shut the angry voices out.

*

My candle flame faltered in a cup;
    we were stood outside the barracks in a line
chanting in rhythm, calling for a stop
    to strip searches for the Armagh women.

The proof that Jesus was a Derry man?
    Thirty-three, unemployed and living with his mother,
the old joke ran. While half the town
    were queuing at the broo, the fortunate others

bent to the task of typing out the cheques.
    Boom! We'd jump at another explosion,
windows buckling in their frames, and next
      you could view the smouldering omission

in a row of shops, the missing tooth
      in a street. Gerry Adams' mouth
was out of sync in the goldfish bowl
      of the TV screen, our dubious link

with the world. Each summer, one by one,
      my sisters upped and crossed the water,
armed with a grant from the government
      – the Butler system's final flowers –

until my own turn came about:
      I watched that place grow small before
the plane ascended through the cloud
      and I could not see it clearly any more.

John Burnside

History

St Andrews: West Sands; September 2001

Today
        as we flew the kites
– the sand spinning off in ribbons along the beach
and that gasoline smell from Leuchars gusting across
the golf links;
                the tide far out
and quail-grey in the distance;
                                        people
jogging, or stopping to watch
as the war planes cambered and turned
in the morning light –

today
        – with the news in my mind, and the muffled dread
of what may come –

                        I knelt down in the sand
with Lucas
            gathering shells
and pebbles
            finding evidence of life in all this
driftwork:
            snail shells; shreds of razorfish;
smudges of weed and flesh on tideworn stone.

At times I think what makes us who we are
is neither kinship nor our given states
but something lost between the world we own
and what we dream about behind the names

on days like this
                    our lines raised in the wind
our bodies fixed and anchored to the shore

and though we are confined by property
what tethers us to gravity and light
has most to do with distance and the shapes
we find in water
                    reading from the book
of silt and tides
                    the rose or petrol blue
of jellyfish and sea anemone
combining with a child's
first nakedness.

Sometimes I am dizzy with the fear
of losing everything – the sea, the sky,
all living creatures, forests, estuaries:
we trade so much to know the virtual
we scarcely register the drift and tug
of other bodies
                    scarcely apprehend
the moment as it happens: shifts of light
and weather
                    and the quiet, local forms
of history: the fish lodged in the tide
beyond the sands;
                    the long insomnia
of ornamental carp in public parks
captive and bright
                    and hung in their own
slow-burning
                    transitive gold;
                            jamjars of spawn
and sticklebacks
                    or goldfish carried home

from fairgrounds
        to the hum of radio

but this is the problem: how to be alive
in all this gazed-upon and cherished world
and do no harm

        a toddler on a beach
sifting wood and dried weed from the sand
and puzzled by the pattern on a shell

his parents on the dune slacks with a kite
plugged into the sky
        all nerve and line

patient; afraid; but still, through everything
attentive to the irredeemable.

Matthew Caley

Eight Ways Of Looking At Lakes

1

From afar, like Ishtar, aloof
on some spectacular limestone outcrop,
through binoculars. You'll be suffering from a headache
beyond the reach of *Aspirin*. It is a headache-coloured sky
and the lake itself is a grey headache, an undistinguished lozenge,
part of a panoramic, cinemascopic sweep,
but boring beneath the sky's distemper,
small.

2

Imagine yourself a minor Lakeland poet,
far from his sister's tussock, plucking an albatross, nursing the itch
of syphilis. With his laudanum-phial and, of course,
his vellum-bound volume of verse. Things can only
get better after this.
Or worse.

3

Close-up. In sunshine. With everything holiday-brochure bright,
airbrushed even. Even. Catch the surface-spangles, gyres, spirals,
silvery ring-pulls, rivets, all chainmail-linked and glinting. Think
of the importance of surfaces. The planes of people's faces.
Be satisfied with shallows. Here clouds are mountains,
mountains clouds and sheeted lakes, inscrutable, mirror both.
For the adventurous, dip your toe halfway
up your toenail. For the gifted – get walking.

4*a*

Read W. H. Auden's *Lakes* [from *Bucolics*] and know all there is to know.
Almost. When you have finished, check the Ordinance Survey Map
of his face. Find solace in each fissure. Wallow.

4*b*

An ankle-deep paddle. We are 70% water ourselves. Little lopsided
waking lakes. Hardly amniotic. Hardly baptismal. Though watch out
for suddenly sepulchral doves that come and go
in a tin-flash. And don't forget your socks
busy sunbathing on the bank.

5

Skinny-dipping. Let the salt support you. Think how many salt tears
would constitute a lake. That cold gasp as lakewater hits your groin.
Dippings, siftings, bits floating off. Your umbilical now knotted
and not in service. Sun-spangles on your cellulite
and your runny, foreshortened legs, thalidomide in rivulets.
Drift off, a jungle-raft to Samarkand and

6

have sex like waterbabies spawning in the spray.
The more professional can water-ski or analyse the wave-raked silt
replete with collective guilt and plastic goggles. Find the greeny-blue
bodies of underage boys and girls barely recognisable
from the local Echo or Star. Lapping darkness. The moiré effect
of bubbles.
Deep, deep. You are diving too deep.

7

The one rule is 'everything ends'.
You now have a choice between the bottom or the bends.

8

This is the bottom. Grey-blue, billowing. Krakens, crud.
Long-missed Masons, rust. An underwater city of muffled bells
malingering beyond. Water or land. No-one can tell which is which.
When you finally set foot in Atlantis
its dust is dry to the touch.

Vahni Capildeo

Stalker

for KM Grant

He waits. Without knowing me,
he waits. The tips of branches,
edible and winey, bring
spring by suggestion to him
who in autumn dawn, eager,
with wet knees, disregards me,
being drawn by me. He waits
and in me he waits. I branch,
the form is branching, it bounds
like sight from dark to bright, back
again. The form is from me:
it is him, poem, stag, first sight
and most known. In him I wait:
(when he falls) needs must (hot heap),
nothing left over (treelike
no longer) nor forlorn: we're
totalled.

Anne Carson

God's Justice

In the beginning there were days set aside for various tasks.
On the day He was to create justice
God got involved in making a dragonfly

and lost track of time.
It was about two inches long
with turquoise dots all down its back like Lauren Bacall.

God watched it bend its tiny wire elbows
as it set about cleaning the transparent case of its head.
The eye globes mounted on the case

rotated this way and that
as it polished every angle.
Inside the case

which was glassy black like the windows of a downtown bank
God could see the machinery humming
and He watched the hum

travel all the way down turquoise dots to the end of the tail
and breathe off as light.
Its black wings vibrated in and out.

Ciaran Carson

Alibi

Remorselessly, in fields and forests, on street corners,
　　on the eternal
Altar of the bed, murder is done. Was I there? I
　　stared into the terminal

Of my own mirrored pupil, and saw my eye denying it,
　　like one hand
Washing clean the other. Where was I then? Everybody
　　wears the same Cain brand

Emblazoned on their foreheads. I saw the deed and what
　　it led to. Heard the shriek
As well. And then my eyes were decommissioned by the knife.
　　But I saw him last week,

And I know he is amongst us. And no, I can't tell his
　　name. What name would you
Make up for murderers of their own childhood, who
　　believe lies to be true?

The lovers enter the marrowbone of a madman and succumb
　　slowly in their pit
Of lime. A croaking black unkindness of ravens has
　　cloaked it

With a counterfeit of corpses. All our words were in vain.
　　What flag are we supposed
To raise above the citadel? Where should we go? All
　　the roads are closed.

O ubiquitous surveillant God, we are accomplices to
    all assassinations.
Gag me, choke me, strangle me, and tell me that there
    are no further destinations.

And finally, it must be left unsaid that those not born
    to this, our vampire family,
Sleep soundly in their beds: they have the final alibi.

Kate Clanchy

War Poetry

The class has dropped its books. The janitor's
disturbed some wasps, broomed the nest
straight off the roof. It lies outside, exotic
as a fallen planet, a burst city of the poor;
its newsprint halls, its ashen, tiny rooms
all open to the air. The insects' buzz
is low-key as a smart machine. They group,
regroup, in stacks and coils, advance
and cross like pulsing points on radar screens.

And though the boys have shaven heads
and football strips, and would, they swear,
enlist at once, given half a chance,
march down Owen's darkening lanes
to join the lads and stuff the Boche –
they don't rush out to pike the nest,
or lap the yard with grapeshot faces.
They watch the wasps through glass,
silently, abashed, the way we all watch war.

Gillian Clarke

Anorexic

My father's sister,
the one who died
before there was a word for it,
was fussy with her food.
'Eat up,' they'd say to me,
ladling a bowl with warning.

What I remember's
how she'd send me to the dairy,
taught me to take cream,
the standing gold.
Where the jug dipped
I saw its blue-milk skin
before the surface healed.

Breath held, tongue between teeth,
I carried in the cream,
brimmed, level,
parallel, I knew,
with that other, hidden horizon
of the earth's deep
ungleaming water-table.

And she, more often than not half-dressed,
stockings, a slip, a Chinese kimono,
would warm the cream, pour it
with crumbled melting cheese
over a delicate white cauliflower,
or field mushrooms
steaming in porcelain,

then watch us eat, relishing,
smoking her umpteenth cigarette,
glamorous, perfumed, starved,
and going to die.

Wendy Cope

Two Cures for Love

1 Don't see him. Don't phone or write a letter.
2 The easy way: get to know him better.

Robert Crawford

Ferrari

Student poser, Presbyterian swami,
When Being and Nothingness ruled the Kelvin Way,

I rebelled by carrying a rolled umbrella
To lectures. I never finished *La Nausée*.

Chaperoned through suburbs by my virginity,
My act of Existential Choice was pie,

Beans and chips at Glasgow's boil-in-the-bag
Student Ref. Couscous? I'd rather have died.

Nightlife was homelife, the tick-tock soothe
Of a bowling club clock, long darning needles' hint

Of suture, so homely and sharp;
Each birthday, a wrapped after-dinner mint.

So, years later, graduated to the glassy Minch,
On the Castlebay ferry, leaning over its rail

Where, below us, a harnessed sailor
Sang from a cradle, painting the ship as it sailed,

I knew, stroking your breasts beneath your blouse,
Both being and nothingness. We kissed like a cashless king

And queen who've just splashed out and bought
A Ferrari for the first day of spring.

Allan Crosbie

Manifesto

Our patience will not yield, our resolve will not break.
We will liberate our children's minds.
We will protect their innocent hearts.
Our strong actions will follow our strong words.
The thirsty will drink, the hungry will eat.
We will teach you to believe what you read.

We will teach you to believe what you read.
Our patience will not yield, our resolve will not break.
The thirsty will drink, the hungry will eat.
We will liberate our children's minds.
Our strong actions will follow our strong words.
We will protect their innocent hearts.

We will protect your innocent hearts.
You will learn to believe what you read.
Strong actions will follow these strong words.
Our patience will not yield, our resolve will not break.
We will liberate our children's minds.
The thirsty will drink, the hungry will eat.

The hungry are drunk, the thirsty may eat.
We will not betray their innocent hearts.
We will not enslave our children's minds.
They will never disbelieve what they read.
Our patience will not yield, our resolve will not break.
Strong actions first demand strong words.

Strong actions first demand strong words
like, *If the thirsty drink and the hungry eat*
our patience will not yield, our resolve will not break.
We will not betray the innocent heart
of this manifesto – believe what you read.
Read my lips: we will enslave your children's minds.

To free them, we must enslave your children's minds.
The actions of the strong speak louder than their words –
if you refuse to believe what you read,
the thirsty won't drink, the hungry won't eat.
We will protect our innocent hearts.
We have patience. You will suffer, yield, break.

We will read your hungry minds.
We will break your strong, strong hearts.
You will eat our innocent words.

Kwame Dawes

New Neighbours

and you know there is a path here
which you must find

somehow quietly
and when you find it

keep it to yourself
like a talisman

and simply toe
the line

don't
smudge it.

Imtiaz Dharker

Its face

A woman getting on a plane.
This is how it will happen.
A bird that has stopped singing
on a still road. This is how it will sound.

This cloth belongs to my face.
Who pulled it off?

That day I saw you
as if a window had broken.
Sharp, with edges that could cut
through cloth and skin.

You wrapped my mouth in plastic
and told me to breathe in free air.
This is how it will feel.

I remember heroes.
Figs, dates, a mango.
This food, your enemy's food.
This is how it will taste.

It will not come
slouching out of the ground.
It walks along a street
that has a familiar name.

This is how it will look.
It will have my face.

Michael Donaghy

My Flu

I'd swear blind it's June, 1962.
Oswald's back from Minsk. U2s glide over Cuba.
My cousin's in Saigon. My father's in bed
with my mother. I'm eight and in bed with my flu.
I'd *swear*, but I can't be recalling this sharp reek of Vicks,
the bedroom's fevered wallpaper, the neighbour's TV,
the rain, the tyres' hiss through rain, the rain smell.
This would never stand up in court – I'm asleep.

I'm curled up, shivering, fighting to wake,
but I can't turn my face from the pit in the woods
– snow filling the broken suitcases, a boy curled up,
like me, as if asleep, except he has no eyes.
One of my father's stories from the war
has got behind my face and filmed itself:
the village written off the map, its only witnesses
marched to the trees. Now all the birds fly up at once.

And who filmed *this* for us, a boy asleep in 1962,
his long-forgotten room, his flu, this endless rain,
the skewed fan rattling, the shouts next door?
My fever reaches 104. But suddenly he's here,
I'd swear, all round me, his hand beneath my head
until one world rings truer than the other.

Tishani Doshi

Turning into Men Again

This morning men are returning to the world,
Waiting on the sides of blackened pavements
For a rickshaw to carry them away
On the sharp pins and soles of their dancing feet.

They must go to the houses of their childhoods
To be soothed. They must wait for the wheels
To appear from the thin arm of road.
They must catch the crack in the sky

Where the light shifts from light to dark
To light again, like the body in the first stages of love;
Angering, heightening, spreading:
Bent knees, bent breath.

Now they are moving, changing colours.
Women are standing at the thresholds of doors
Holding jars of oil, buckets of hot water and salt,
Calamine, crushed mint and drink.

Some crawl into their mother's laps,
Collapse against the heavy bosoms of old nannies,
Search for the girl who climbed with them
To the tin roof for the first time.

Inside, in the shadows of pillars,
Fathers and grandfathers are stepping down
From picture frames with secrets on their lips,
Calling the lost in from their voyages.

Jane Draycott

No. 3 *from* Uses for the Thames

'"Feather!" cried the Sheep...'
> Lewis Carroll, *Through the Looking-Glass*

The test was to dip
the needles into the dark
of the swallowing mirror

and by pulling to row
the weight of your own small self
through the silvery jam of its surface

trailing behind in your passing
your very own tale, knitted
extempore from light

and then to lift them,
feathered, ready for flight.

Carol Ann Duffy

Valentine

Not a red rose or a satin heart.

I give you an onion.
It is a moon wrapped in brown paper.
It promises light
like the careful undressing of love.

Here.
It will blind you with tears
like a lover.
It will make your reflection
a wobbling photo of grief.

I am trying to be truthful.

Not a cute card or a kissogram.

I give you an onion.
Its fierce kiss will stay on your lips,
possessive and faithful
as we are,
for as long as we are.

Take it.
Its platinum loops shrink to a wedding-ring,
if you like.
Lethal.
Its scent will cling to your fingers,
cling to your knife.

Ian Duhig

The Lammas Hireling

After the fair, I'd still a light heart
And a heavy purse, he struck so cheap.
And cattle doted on him: in his time
Mine only dropped heifers, fat as cream.
Yields doubled. I grew fond of company
That knew when to shut up. Then one night,

Disturbed from dreams of my dear late wife,
I hunted down her torn voice to his pale form.
Stock-still in the light from the dark lantern,
Stark-naked but for the fox-trap biting his ankle,
I knew him a warlock, a cow with leather horns.
To go into the hare gets you muckle sorrow,

The wisdom runs, muckle care. I levelled
And blew the small hour through his heart.
The moon came out. By its yellow witness
I saw him fur over like a stone mossing.
His lovely head thinned. His top lip gathered.
His eyes rose like bread. I carried him

In a sack that grew lighter at every step
And dropped him from a bridge. There was no
Splash. Now my herd's elf-shot. I don't dream
But spend my nights casting ball from half-crowns
And my days here. Bless me, Father, I have sinned.
It has been an hour since my last confession.

Helen Dunmore

To my nine-year-old self

You must forgive me. Don't look so surprised,
perplexed, and eager to be gone,
balancing on your hands or on the tightrope.
You would rather run than walk, rather climb than run
rather leap from a height than anything.

I have spoiled this body we once shared.
Look at the scars, and watch the way I move,
careful of a bad back or a bruised foot.
Do you remember how, three minutes after waking
we'd jump straight out of the ground floor window
into the summer morning?

That dream we had, no doubt it's as fresh in your mind
as the white paper to write it on.
We made a start, but something else came up –
a baby vole, or a bag of sherbet lemons –
and besides, that summer of ambition
created an ice-lolly factory, a wasp trap
and a den by the cesspit.

I'd like to say that we could be friends
but the truth is we have nothing in common
beyond a few shared years. I won't keep you then.
Time to pick rosehips for tuppence a pound,
time to hide down scared lanes
from men in cars after girl-children,

or to lunge out over the water
on a rope that swings from that tree
long buried in housing –
but no, I shan't cloud your morning. God knows
I have fears enough for us both –

I leave you in an ecstasy of concentration
slowly peeling a ripe scab from your knee
to taste it on your tongue.

UA Fanthorpe

Atlas

There is a kind of love called maintenance,
Which stores the WD40 and knows when to use it;

Which checks the insurance, and doesn't forget
The milkman; which remembers to plant bulbs;

Which answers letters; which knows the way
The money goes; which deals with dentists

And Road Fund Tax and meeting trains,
And postcards to the lonely; which upholds

The permanently ricketty elaborate
Structures of living; which is Atlas.

And maintenance is the sensible side of love,
Which knows what time and weather are doing
To my brickwork; insulates my faulty wiring;
Laughs at my dryrotten jokes; remembers
My need for gloss and grouting; which keeps
My suspect edifice upright in air,
As Atlas did the sky.

Paul Farley

Liverpool Disappears for a Billionth of a Second

Shorter than the blink inside a blink
the National Grid will sometimes make, when you'll
turn to a room and say: *Was that just me?*

People sitting down for dinner don't feel
their chairs taken away / put back again
much faster than that trick with tablecloths.

A train entering the Olive Mount cutting
shudders, but not a single passenger
complains when it pulls in almost on time.

The birds feel it, though, and if you see
starlings in shoal, seagulls abandoning
cathedral ledges, or a mob of pigeons

lifting from a square as at gunfire,
be warned, it may be happening, but then
those sensitive to bat-squeak in the backs

of necks, who claim to hear the distant roar
of comets on the turn – these may well smile
at a world restored, in one piece; though each place

where mineral Liverpool goes wouldn't believe
what hit it: all that sandstone out to sea
or meshed into the quarters of Cologne.

I've felt it a few times when I've gone home,
if anything, more often now I'm old,
and the gaps between get shorter all the time.

Vicki Feaver

Judith

Wondering how a good woman can murder
I enter the tent of Holofernes,
holding in one hand his long oiled hair
and in the other, raised above
his sleeping, wine-flushed face,
his falchion with its unsheathed
curved blade. And I feel a rush
of tenderness, a longing
to put down my weapon, to lie
sheltered and safe in a warrior's
fumy sweat, under the emerald stars
of his purple and gold canopy,
to melt like a sweet on his tongue
to nothing. And I remember the glare
of the barley field; my husband
pushing away the sponge I pressed
to his burning head; the stubble
puncturing my feet as I ran,
flinging myself on a body
that was already cooling
and stiffening; and the nights
when I lay on the roof – my emptiness
like the emptiness of a temple
with the doors kicked in; and the mornings
when I rolled in the ash of the fire
just to be touched and dirtied
by something. And I bring my blade
down on his neck – and it's easy
like slicing through fish.
And I bring it down again,
cleaving the bone.

Duncan Forbes

Recension Day

Unburn the boat, rebuild the bridge,
Reconsecrate the sacrilege,
Unspill the milk, decry the tears,
Turn back the clock, relive the years,
Replace the smoke inside the fire,
Unite fulfilment with desire,
Undo the done, gainsay the said,
Revitalise the buried dead,
Revoke the penalty and clause,
Reconstitute unwritten laws,
Repair the heart, untie the tongue,
Change faithless old to hopeful young,
Inure the body to disease
And help me to forget you please.

Linda France

Cooking with Blood

Last night I dreamt of Delia Smith again –
smoked buckling simmering on the horizon,
that old Doverhouse moon stuffing the dumpling
of a crackling sky. She played en papillote

for just long enough to sweat me garlicky.
After I'd peppered her liver, stuffed her goose
and dogfished her tender loins, she was pâté
in my hands. She got all mulligatawny

so I tossed her into a nine herb salad
of Hintlesham. She was my Russian herring,
my giblet stock. We danced the ossobuco;
her belly kedgeree, her breasts prosciutto.

I tongue-casseroled her ear she was my Queen
of Puddings and wouldn't we sausage lots
of little quichelets, a platter of sprats
we'd name Béarnaise, Mortadella, Bara brith.

But when the trout hit the tabasco, it turned out
she was only pissaladière, garam
masala as a savoyard. Arrowroot.
Just another dip in love with crudités.

And I've stroganoffed with too many of them.
I chopped home to my own bloater paste and triped
myself into a carcass. No wonder I woke up
with scarlet farts, dried blood under my fingernails,

dreaming of Delia, her oxtail, again.

Matthew Francis

The Ornamental Hermit

Not really ornamental, a white figure
you might glimpse from the drive, deep in the beech woods,
as you were making your way towards the house,
standing so still he might have been a long strip
of sunlight on the bark, except that you felt,
not his eyes on you exactly, but his *thoughts*.

Hardly anyone saw him close up. The cook,
who had, said he was wearing a floppy robe
of coarse stuff and looked like a man in a bag,
and a visitor who had come face to face
with what appeared to be a nightgowned person
supposed he was mad or walking in his sleep.

No one could agree on his age. The footman
who left last night's jellied fowl and potatoes
beside his sandbank grotto in the morning
would say, after a long pause, he thought the chap
wore spectacles but he stayed in the shadows
hunched over his Bible. They were not to speak.

He was a lover who had renounced the world
or else he had been promised a thousand pounds
if he could live for seven years in the cave
that had been scooped out for him, rising at dawn,
then brooding the whole day over the hourglass,
at night praying or reading by candlelight.

Hermits were all the rage these days but this one
could not have been laid on as an ornament
for houseparties. Some of the guests went so far
as to doubt his existence, or at least claimed
that he had long ago climbed the wall, leaving
his implements in the slowly filling hole.

But it was like this. There are times when a man
must grasp where he is living. It's not enough
any more to lie under your roof at night
hearing the dry rain, to own all those acres
of dark and dirt, without someone to feel it,
to be in the thick. That's what I paid him for.

Pamela Gillilan

Three Ways to a Silk Shirt

You have to kill for silk
and it's not easy. Those chrysalides
make themselves so private
in their tight shuttles, so safe
that they can dare to lose themselves
to metamorphosis, abandon the known body
and endure who can imagine what liquidity
before another form takes shape.

They must be murdered in the midst
of miracle, their cerements reeled off,
the long continuous thread saved
pliable, unstained, the severing bite
of the emerging moth forestalled.

The method's suffocation –
the oldest way by baking in hot sun;
but this hardens the thread,
makes unwinding a hard labour,
risks soiling by windborne dust,
is wasteful.

Steaming's another way – the plump bolls held
above a boiling cauldron for eight minutes
then for eight weeks spread out to dry
well-aired, so that the corpse in the shroud
desiccates slowly, leaves no stain;
but sometimes the chrysalis survives.

Surest is heated air. A single day exposed
to the technology of fans and ducts, the flow
of arid currents, and the pupa's void,
a juiceless chitin spindle shrivelled back
from the close wrappings drawn and spun
out of its former self – now to be unwound
and spun again: woven, dyed, cut and sewn,
collared and cuffed.

Alan Gillis

Bulletin from The Daily Mail

You must have seen those Rent Street potheads,
their skin all sweating processed chicken meat:
knives taped to their thighs, blood-red dots for eyes,
stolen shoes like rocketblasters on their feet?

As sure as rainfall, they're at the entrance to the mall,
tattooed necks livid with love bites.
Hooked to mobile phones, they know your way home
and they wait for you in alleyways at night.

They spit on the bus, their fingers are warty,
they set fire to schools, sniff WD40,
they climb any fence, they climb any roof,
they jump on your bonnet and smash your sunroof,

they'll squeeze through your window and creep up your stairs,
they'll leave your comb crawling with their pubic hairs,
they'll crowbar your gold teeth right out of your head,
they excrete on the street, and they don't go to bed.

John Goodby

The Uncles

Uncles, talking the camshaft or the gimbal connected
to a slowly oscillating crank. The Uncles Brickell,
Swarfega kings, enseamed with swarf and scobs, skin
measled with gunmetal but glistening faintly, loud
in the smoke. Lithe and wiry above the lathe, milling out
a cylinder to a given bore. Uncles, pencil-stubs at their ears,
spurning ink, crossing sevens like émigré intellectuals,
measuring in thous and thirty-secondths (scrawled
on torn fag-packets); feinting with slide rules, racing,
but mild not as mild steel. Pockets congested, always. Uncles
with dockets for jobs, corners transparent with grease,
with a light machine oil. Time-served, my Uncles, branch-
ing out into doorhandles, grub-screws and the brass bits
that hold the front of the motor case to the rear flange
of the mounting panel. Release tab. Slightly hard of hearing
now, the Uncles, from the din of the shop, slowly nodding.
Uncles in 'Red Square'; uncles swapping tolerance gauges,
allen keys, telephone numbers, deals and rank commun-
ism. Forefingers describing arcs and cutting angles. White
and milky with coolants and lubricants, mess of order. Never
forgetting to ply a broom after. The missing half-finger, not
really missed any longer, just a banjo-hand gone west. My
Uncles still making a go of mower blades, on the road
at their age; offering cigars at Christmas. Uncanny if
encountered in visors, overalls, confounding nephews
in dignity of their calling, their epoch-stewed tea. Stand
a spoon in all their chamfered years, cut short or long. Uncles
immortal in the welding shed, under neon, lounge
as the vast doors slide to a cool blue dusk. My Uncles.

Lavinia Greenlaw

A World Where News Travelled Slowly

It could take from Monday to Thursday
and three horses. The ink was unstable,
the characters cramped, the paper tore where it creased.
Stained with the leather and sweat of its journey,
the envelope absorbed each climatic shift,
as well as the salt and grease of the rider
who handed it over with a four-day chance
that by now things were different and while the head
had to listen, the heart could wait.

Semaphore was invented at a time of revolution;
the judgement of swing in a vertical arm.
News travelled letter by letter, along a chain of towers,
each built within telescopic distance of the next.
The clattering mechanics of the six-shutter telegraph
still took three men with all their variables
added to those of light and weather,
to read, record and pass the message on.

Now words are faster, smaller, harder
...*we're almost talking in one another's arms.*
Coded and squeezed, what chance has my voice
to reach your voice unaltered and to leave no trace?
Nets tighten across the sky and the sea bed.
When London made contact with New York,
there were such fireworks, City Hall caught light.
It could have burned to the ground.

Thom Gunn

Lament

Your dying was a difficult enterprise.
First, petty things took up your energies,
The small but clustering duties of the sick,
Irritant as the cough's dry rhetoric.
Those hours of waiting for pills, shot, X-ray
Or test (while you read novels two a day)
Already with a kind of clumsy stealth
Distanced you from the habits of your health.
    In hope still, courteous still, but tired and thin,
You tried to stay the man that you had been,
Treating each symptom as a mere mishap
Without import. But then the spinal tap.
It brought a hard headache, and when night came
I heard you wake up from the same bad dream
Every half-hour with the same short cry
Of mild outrage, before immediately
Slipping into the nightmare once again
Empty of content but the drip of pain.
No respite followed: though the nightmare ceased,
Your cough grew thick and rich, its strength increased.
Four nights, and on the fifth we drove you down
To the Emergency Room. That frown, that frown:
I'd never seen such rage in you before
As when they wheeled you through the swinging door.
For you knew, rightly, they conveyed you from
Those normal pleasures of the sun's kingdom
The hedonistic body basks within
And takes for granted – summer on the skin,
Sleep without break, the moderate taste of tea
In a dry mouth. You had gone on from me
As if your body sought out martyrdom

In the far Canada of a hospital room.
Once there, you entered fully the distress
And long pale rigours of the wilderness.
A gust of morphine hid you. Back in sight
You breathed through a segmented tube, fat, white,
Jammed down your throat so that you could not speak.
How thin the distance made you. In your cheek
One day, appeared the true shape of your bone
No longer padded. Still your mind, alone,
Explored this emptying intermediate
State for what holds and rests were hidden in it.
You wrote us messages on a pad, amused
At one time that you had your nurse confused
Who, seeing you reconciled after four years
With your grey father, both of you in tears,
Asked if this was at last your 'special friend'
(the one you waited for until the end).
'She sings,' you wrote, 'a Philippine folk song
To wake me in the morning…It is long
And very pretty.' Grabbing at detail
To furnish this bare ledge toured by the gale,
On which you lay, bed restful as a knife,
You tried, tried hard, to make of it a life
Thick with the complicating circumstance
Your thoughts might fasten on. It had been chance
Always till now that had filled up the moment
With live specifics your hilarious comment
Discovered as it went along; and fed,
Laconic, quick, wherever it was led.
You improvised upon your own delight.
I think back to the scented summer night
We talked between our sleeping bags, below
A molten field of stars five years ago:
I was so tickled by your mind's light touch
I couldn't sleep, you made me laugh too much,
Though I was tired and begged you to leave off.

Now you were tired, and yet not tired enough
– Still hungry for the great world you were losing
Steadily in no season of your choosing –
And when at last the whole death was assured,
Drugs having failed, and when you had endured
Two weeks of an abominable constraint,
You faced it equably, without complaint,
Unwhimpering, but not at peace with it.
You'd lived as if your time was infinite:
You were not ready and not reconciled,
Feeling as uncompleted as a child
Till you had shown the world what you could do
In some ambitious role to be worked through,
A role your need for it had half-defined,
But never wholly, even in your mind.
You lacked the necessary ruthlessness,
The soaring meanness that pinpoints success.
We loved that lack of self-love, and your smile,
Rueful, at your own silliness.
                                        Meanwhile,
Your lungs collapsed, and the machine, unstrained,
Did all your breathing now. Nothing remained
But death by drowning on an inland sea
Of your own fluids, which it seemed could be
Kindly forestalled by drugs. Both could and would:
Nothing was said, everything understood,
At least by us. Your own concerns were not
Long-term, precisely, when they gave the shot
– You made local arrangements to the bed
And pulled a pillow round beside your head.
   And so you slept, and died, your skin gone grey,
Achieving your completeness, in a way.

Outdoors next day, I was dizzy from a sense
Of being ejected with some violence
From vigil in a white and distant spot
Where I was numb, into this garden plot

Too warm, too close, and not enough like pain.
I was delivered into time again
– The variations that I live among
Where your long body too used to belong
And where the still bush is minutely active.
You never thought your body was attractive,
Though others did, and yet you trusted it
And must have loved its fickleness a bit
Since it was yours and gave you what it could,
Till near the end it let you down for good,
Its blood hospitable to those guests who
Took over by betraying it into
The greatest of its inconsistencies
This difficult, tedious, painful enterprise.

Jen Hadfield

Definitions

after Jerome Rothenberg

The Brisket
This cinched consonant, hunched muscle in a yellow
simmet, could also signify a journey. It could feed a family,
or stop the third gob of the three-headed dog. You bind it
to your stick as you set off for the Underworld. Browned, it
melts into punctuated mud, is thick fuel for migrations,
night flights you can't remember. It's a passing madness in
the cat; it makes him a round-eyed bawling bob-cat. It
squirms under the distal phalanges of a splayed hand. It
bucks the bite of the knife. It foams fat.

The Cat
is sleeping very deeply now it's spring been off his head
hunting rabbits all night, in the far-out stones and discoball
eyes of the clifftop crö. His days a kind of stoned remission:
heart-beat irregular, muscles leaping violently in sleep. The
wet bracelet of his mouth unlatched; chattering a little; his
eyelids half-open. His furry buffers nicely spread all about
him; nicely buffered by fat and fur all round.

Equus Primus
as if some god having turned out another batch of
underdone horses (thin as leaves, dappled like leaves) freed
them on the hill to flicker like a thicket of hornbeam and
willow; set down his cutter and balled the waste dough.
Thence this tribe of blackened emoticons, tough as plugs.

The Word 'Died'

It's a cliff-sided stack: sheer, almost an island. A human
can't stand upon that high, tilted pasture but life crowds its
cliffs: sheep and nesting maas, the waste-not plants of
heath and moor. You hear the waves breaking but can't see
them. You shrink down into yourself as you reach the edge:
getting your head around where you are. It's marvellous.
It's aweful. It is always on. Like a massive *and* unfolding its
wings, and mantling. It was here all along, reached by
Shirva and the derelict mills; turf sweating in the hot,
midgy smirr.

The Mackerel

At once, the three hooks chime. The skin is as supple as the
skin on boiled milk and the eye a hard, roundel pane. It is
or it isn't wormy, it tastes of hot blood and earth, tastes of
long-awaited rain, winter lightning and summer thunder.
Heart-throb; mud-coloured; the cooked flesh is tarnish. The
oatmeal crisp. It tastes of steak, it tastes of cream.

The Northern Lights

– but yes, now you pull over – after the headlights, a raw
shifting glare. I've taken them often for a moon behind
cloud. An ambiguous rustling, yes, maybe listening in, when
being overheard is your greatest fear. Like an infection of the
lymph, a shooting-up – that single, white flare.

The Orange

Bloated, swollen with sea-water, it's a boast, fraught with
salt syrup. It forces your fingers apart and makes much of
itself. It is über, *aaber*. A very straining round real orange,
stinking of orange and the sea; stinking of stale cologne.
The sea returns whatever you give it, more so, realler.
Headachy wax! It rolls down the sand into the foam. It
spins at the crest of the breaker!

The Parents
are on the pale brisk longbusy birdbrushed billows of the
equinoctial sea. Without them is a long, unhappy holiday.
Who else gives a shit about your shitty knee? You're
breathless at the thought of them all-night on the sea.
Blithely they step into its bright pale machinery. They
make mandalas of quartz and limpet-shells, hide cash under
a hairbrush, vanish with their luggage as pixies might. The
pillows squared to each other. The sheets pulled tight.

The Pig
is as they say, very human, though our bellies do not
resemble her belly, which is like one of the papyriform
columns at Luxor. Nor can we liken our nipples to her
torment of buttons, our ears to her arums. Our lugs are
unfringed with soft, blonde baleen. But her fetishes: her
forked stick; her devilish loop of rotted rope. Her precious
rasher of chicken wire. Her tired, human eye. Her
constancy as a conspirator.

The Puffballs
Somebody's watching. Two toughened eyeballs propped
behind you on the turf.

The Puffin
A tangled marionette, strings of jerked sinew. Summer's
end, the derelict burrow, a ring of dirty down. An
arabesque of smelly bone, meat for flies and the darling
turf. The head may be full of meat; the large beak, faded: a
Fabergé egg.

The Road to the North Light
It weeps tar from tender parts like frogskin. Thin, mobile
muscles squirm under your soles as it bears you across the
Hill Dyke on a current of cool air, the bed of an invisible
river. It has heather and tormentil, not dandelion but catsear.
It has a creep over a precipice; it has sorrel, parched and tiny.
It carries you above the white and lilac sea; it switchbacks,
and turns you before the sun like a sacrifice.

The Slater
We alone among the creatures are known to imagine our
own minds. Like this woodlouse on the kitchen floor. It
perceives you, rears and comes about. Stroking with its
spurred feet a precipitate of dried soup, a peel hovering
above its own shadow.

The Waxcaps
Someone was carried across this field, bleeding steadily.

Tony Harrison

A Cold Coming

> *'A cold coming we had of it.'*
> TS Eliot, 'Journey of the Magi'

I saw the charred Iraqi lean
towards me from bomb-blasted screen,

his windscreen wiper like a pen
ready to write down thoughts for men,

his windscreen wiper like a quill
he's reaching for to make his will.

I saw the charred Iraqi lean
like someone made of Plasticine

as though he'd stopped to ask the way
and this is what I heard him say:

'Don't be afraid I've picked on you
for this exclusive interview.

Isn't it your sort of poet's task
to find words for this frightening mask?

If that gadget that you've got records
words from such scorched vocal chords,

press RECORD before some dog
devours me mid-monologue.'

So I held the shaking microphone
closer to the crumbling bone:

'I read the news of three wise men
who left their sperm in nitrogen,

three foes of ours, three wise Marines
with sample flasks and magazines,

three wise soldiers from Seattle
who banked their sperm before the battle.

Did No. 1 say: God be thanked
I've got my precious semen banked.

And No. 2: O praise the Lord
my last best shot is safely stored.

And No. 3: Praise be to God
I left my wife my frozen wad?

So if their fate was to be gassed
at least they thought their name would last,

and though cold corpses in Kuwait
they could by proxy procreate.

Excuse a skull half roast, half bone
for using such a scornful tone.

It may seem out of all proportion
but I wish I'd taken their precaution.

They seemed the masters of their fate
with wisely jarred ejaculate.

Was it a propaganda coup
to make us think they'd cracked death too,

disinformation to defeat us
with no post-mortem millilitres?

Symbolic billions in reserve
made me, for one, lose heart and nerve.

On Saddam's pay we can't afford
to go and get our semen stored.

Sad to say that such high tech's
uncommon here. We're stuck with sex.

If you can conjure up and stretch
your imagination (and not retch)

the image of me beside my wife
closely clasped creating life…'

(I let the unfleshed skull unfold
a story I'd been already told,

and idly tried to calculate
the content of ejaculate:

the sperm in one ejaculation
equals the whole Iraqi nation

times, roughly, let's say, 12.5
though that .5's not now alive.

Let's say the sperms were an amount
so many times the body count,

2,500 times at least
(but let's wait till the toll's released!).

Whichever way Death seems outflanked
by one tube of cold bloblings banked.

Poor bloblings, maybe you've been blessed
with, of all fates possible, the best

according to Sophocles i.e.
'the best of fates is not to be'

a philosophy that's maybe bleak
for any but an ancient Greek

but difficult these days to escape
when spoken to by such a shape.

When you see men brought to such states
who wouldn't want that 'best of fates'

or in the world of Cruise and Scud
not go kryonic if he could,

spared the normal human doom
of having made it through the womb?)

He heard my thoughts and stopped the spool:
'I never thought life futile, fool!

Though all Hell began to drop
I never wanted life to stop.

I was filled with such a yearning
to stay in life as I was burning,

such a longing to be beside
my wife in bed before I died,

and, most, to have engendered there
a child untouched by war's despair.

So press RECORD! I want to reach
the warring nations with my speech.

Don't look away! I know it's hard
to keep regarding one so charred,

so disfigured by unfriendly fire
and think it once burned with desire.

Though fire has flayed off half my features
they once were like my fellow creatures',

till some screen-gazing crop-haired boy
from Iowa or Illinois,

equipped by ingenious technophile
put paid to my paternal smile

and made the face you see today
an armature half-patched with clay,

an icon framed, a looking glass
for devotees of "kicking ass",

a mirror that returns the gaze
of victors on their victory days

and in the end stares out the watcher
who ducks behind his headline: GOTCHA!

or behind the flag-bedecked page 1
of the true to bold-type-setting SUN!

I doubt victorious Greeks let Hector
join their feast as spoiling spectre,

and who'd want to sour the children's joy
in Iowa or Illinois

or ageing mothers overjoyed
to find their babies weren't destroyed?

But cabs beflagged with SUN front pages
don't help peace in future ages.

Stars and Stripes in sticky paws
may sow the seeds for future wars.

Each Union Jack the kids now wave
may lead them later to the grave.

But praise the Lord and raise the banner
(excuse a skull's sarcastic manner!)

Desert Rat and Desert Stormer
without scars and (maybe) trauma,

the semen-bankers are all back
to sire their children in their sack.

With seed sown straight from the sower
dump second-hand spermatozoa!

Lie that you saw me and I smiled
to see the soldier hug his child.

Lie and pretend that I excuse
my bombing by B52s,

pretend I pardon and forgive
that they still do and I don't live,

pretend they have the burnt man's blessing
and then, maybe, I'm spared confessing

that only fire burnt out the shame
of things I'd done in Saddam's name,

the deaths, the torture and the plunder
the black clouds all of us are under.

Say that I'm smiling and excuse
the Scuds we launched against the Jews.

Pretend I've got the imagination
to see the world beyond one nation.

That's your job, poet, to pretend
I want my foe to be my friend.

It's easier to find such words
for this dumb mask like baked dogturds.

So lie and say the charred man smiled
to see the soldier hug his child.

This gaping rictus once made glad
a few old hearts back in Baghdad,

hearts growing older by the minute
as each truck comes without me in it.

I've met you though, and had my say
which you've got taped. Now go away.'

I gazed at him and he gazed back
staring right through me to Iraq.

Facing the way the charred man faced
I saw the frozen phial of waste,

a test-tube frozen in the dark,
crib and Kaaba, sacred Ark,

a pilgrimage of Cross and Crescent
the chilled suspension of the Present.

Rainbows seven shades of black
curved from Kuwait back to Iraq,

and instead of gold the frozen crock's
crammed with Mankind on the rocks,

the congealed geni who won't thaw
until the World renounces War,

cold spunk meticulously jarred
never to be charrer or the charred,

a bottled Bethlehem of this come-
curdling Cruise/Scud-cursed millennium.

I went. I pressed REWIND and PLAY
and I heard the charred man say:

David Harsent

The Curator

Everything under glass and still as stone. Where an item
was out on loan, a photograph gave its likeness: at a
glance you'd own they were little but horn and bone.
'I'm busy just now,' he said, 'why not go on alone? You
can't get easily lost. Those arrows will bring you home.'

> *This is the razor that turned on its owner,*
> *this is the finger that fired the first shot,*
> *this is the flower that poisoned its wearer,*
> *this is the riddle that started the rot.*

But when I turned the corner, he was there; of course he
was. 'Aren't we a pair?' he laughed, as if climbing the
stair in step, as if breathing that mouldy air, might make
us sudden partners in Truth-or-Dare. He thumbed the
catalogue; the sheer size of it made me stare: the weight
of loss. 'Is it something particular?' As if he didn't
know. 'Is it something awry or unfair?'

> *This is the poodle that bit Aristotle,*
> *this is the tongue with the strawberry wart,*
> *this is the rattle they found in the shtetl,*
> *this is the cutie who wouldn't abort.*

He stood at the door to see me off, and wore the cloths of
frailty like the Godless poor: which fooled me not one
bit. 'You've seen damn-all, you know, but if you're sure –'
He snicked the ID off my coat and tore the lapel a token
inch. 'A souvenir...' Now I no longer wore my face and
name. 'It's queer,' he shook my hand, 'this way or that,
they all come back for more.'

This is the tumour that grew like a rumour,
this is the rafter and this is the rope,
this is the drama that buried the dreamer,
this is the hope beyond hope beyond hope.

Seamus Heaney

The Blackbird of Glanmore

On the grass when I arrive,
Filling the stillness with life,
But ready to scare off
At the very first wrong move.
In the ivy when I leave.

It's you, blackbird, I love.

I park, pause, take heed.
Breathe. Just breathe and sit
And lines I once translated
Come back: 'I want away
To the house of death, to my father

Under the low clay roof.'

And I think of one gone to him,
A little stillness dancer –
Haunter-son, lost brother –
Cavorting through the yard,
So glad to see me home,

My homesick first term over.

And think of a neighbour's words
Long after the accident:
'Yon bird on the shed roof,
Up on the ridge for weeks –
I said nothing at the time

But I never liked yon bird.'

The automatic lock
Clunks shut, the blackbird's panic
Is shortlived, for a second
I've a bird's eye view of myself,
A shadow on raked gravel

In front of my house of life.

Hedge-hop, I am absolute
For you, your ready talkback,
Your each stand-offish comeback,
Your picky, nervy goldbeak –
On the grass when I arrive,

In the ivy when I leave.

Stuart Henson

The Price

Sometimes it catches when the fumes rise up
among the throbbing lights of cars, or as
you look away to dodge eye-contact with
your own reflection in the carriage-glass;
or in a waiting-room a face reminds you
that the colour supplements have lied
and some have pleasure and some pay the price.
Then all the small securities you built
about your house, your desk, your calendar
are blown like straws; and momentarily,
as if a scent of ivy or the earth
had opened up a childhood door, you pause,
to take the measure of what might have been
against the kind of life you settled for.

WN Herbert

Smirr

The leaves flick past the windows of the train
like feeding swifts: they're scooping up small mouth-
fuls of the midge-like autumn, fleeing south
with the train's hot wake: their feathers are small rain.
'Serein' they could say, where I'm passing through,
then just a sound could link rain with the leaves'
symptom, of being sere. But who deceives
themselves such rhyming leaps knit seasons now?
Some alchemist would get the point at once;
why I, against the leaves' example, try
migrating to my cold roots like a dunce.
Thicker than needles sticking to a fir,
Winter is stitching mists of words with chance,
like smears of myrrh, like our small rain, our smirr.

Geoffrey Hill

from **The Orchards of Syon**

I

Now there is no due season. Do not
mourn unduly. You have sometimes said
that I project a show more
stressful than delightful. Watch my hands
confabulate their shadowed rhetoric,
gestures of benediction; maledictions
by arrangement. For us there is
no deadline, neither for stand nor standoff.
I can prolong the act at times
to rival Augustine, this shutter
play among words, befitting
a pact with light, the contra-Faustian heist
from judgement to mercy.
I shall promote our going and coming,
as shadows, in expressive light; take
my belief, if only through a process
taxing salvation — may I proceed? —
not merely to divert with faith and fiction,
to ease peregrination, what a life!
Has it ever been staged
seriously outside Spain, I mean
La vida es sueño? Tell me, is this the way
to the Orchards of Syon
where I left you thinking I would return?

Selima Hill

Please Can I Have a Man

Please can I have a man who wears corduroy.
Please can I have a man
who knows the names of 100 different roses;
who doesn't mind my absent-minded rabbits
wandering in and out
as if they own the place,
who makes me creamy curries from fresh lemon-grass,
who walks like Belmondo in *A Bout de Souffle*;
who sticks all my carefully-selected postcards –
sent from exotic cities
he doesn't expect to come with me to,
but would if I asked, which I will do –
with nobody else's, up on his bedroom wall,
starting with Ivy, the Famous Diving Pig,
whose picture, in action, I bought ten copies of;
who talks like Belmondo too, with lips as smooth
and tightly-packed as chocolate-coated
(*melting* chocolate) peony buds;
who knows that piling himself stubbornly on top of me
like a duvet stuffed with library books and shopping-bags
is all too easy: please can I have a man
who is not prepared to do that.
Who is not prepared to say I'm 'pretty' either.
Who, when I come trotting in from the bathroom
like a squealing freshly-scrubbed piglet
that likes nothing better than a binge
of being affectionate and undisciplined and uncomplicated,
opens his arms like a trough for me to dive into.

Ellen Hinsey

XVII Correspondences:
Aphorisms Regarding Impatience

1.
Mythologies of the End
Each century believing itself poised as if on the edge of time.

2.
The Meaning of Impatience
Restlessness in time. To imagine that which is not swiftly accomplished will never be fulfilled.

3.
Displaced Envy
Unable to initiate creation, or manage civilization: the drive to engineer *decreation* with perfection.

4.
Perplexing Instincts
The division of the spirit between advancement and abandon.

5.
The Attraction of the Apocalypse
To control with absolute certainty one thing. And for it to be the last.

6.
Fragile Vector
The intersection where civilization and perseverance meet.

7.
The Effort of Civilization
Miraculous labor. Each day Sisyphus rolling his rock uphill against the accidental nature of mankind.

8.
Not a Solution
To draw into question Sisyphus's task.

9.
Accepting Negative Inevitability
Intellectual sleepwalking. The ethical self abdicating *affirmation* for the temptation of *renunciation*.

10.
Deviant Logic
To reject contingencies of disaster. To glean *possibility* from the crevices of *improbability*.

11.
What is at Stake
The fragile geometry of the world held in hostage.

12.
Not the End
A type of grace: waiting in impatience to see that, from now until the far edge of always, *nothing happens*.

Sarah Howe

Tame

> '*It is more profitable to raise geese than daughters.*'
> Chinese proverb

This is the tale of the woodsman's daughter. Born with a box
      of ashes set beside the bed,
in case. Before the baby's first cry, he rolled her face into the cinders –
      held it. Weak from the bloom
of too-much-blood, the new mother tried to stop his hand. He dragged
      her out into the yard, flogged her
with the usual branch. If it was magic in the wood, they never
      said, but she began to change:

her scar-ridged back, beneath his lashes, toughened to a rind; it split
      and crusted into bark. Her prone
knees dug in the sandy ground and rooted, questing for water,
      as her work-grained fingers lengthened
into twigs. The tree – a lychee – he continued to curse as if it
      were his wife – its useless, meagre
fruit. Meanwhile the girl survived. Feathered in greyish ash,
      her face tucked in, a little gosling.

He called her Mei Ming: *No Name.* She never learned to speak. Her life
      maimed by her father's sorrow.
For grief is a powerful thing – even for objects never conceived.
      He should have dropped her down
the well. Then at least he could forget. Sometimes when he set
      to work, hefting up his axe
to watch the cleanness of its arc, she butted at his elbow – again,
      again – with her restive head,

till angry, he flapped her from him. But if these silent pleas had
        meaning, neither knew.
The child's only comfort came from nestling under the
        lychee tree. Its shifting branches
whistled her wordless lullabies: the lychees with their watchful eyes,
        the wild geese crossing overhead.
The fruit, the geese. They marked her seasons. She didn't long to join
        the birds, if longing implies

a will beyond the blindest instinct. Then one mid-autumn, she craned
        her neck so far to mark the geese
wheeling through the clouded hills – it kept on stretching – till
        it tapered in a beak. Her pink toes
sprouted webs and claws; her helpless arms found strength
        in wings. The goose daughter
soared to join the arrowed skein: kin linked by a single aim
        and tide, she knew their heading

and their need. They spent that year or more in flight, but where –
        across what sparkling tundral wastes –
I've not heard tell. Some say the fable ended there. But those
        who know the ways of wild geese
know too the obligation to return, to their first dwelling place. Let this
        suffice: late spring. A woodsman
snares a wild goose that spirals clean into his yard – almost like
        it knows. Gripping its sinewed neck

he presses it down into the block, cross-hewn from a lychee trunk.
        A single blow. Profit, loss.

Ted Hughes

Flounders

Was that a happy day? From Chatham
Down at the South end of the Cape, our map
Somebody's optimistic assurance,
We set out to row. We got ourselves
Into mid-channel. The tide was flowing. We hung
Anchored. Northward-pulling, our baited leads
Bounced and bounced the bottom. For three hours –
Two or three sea-robins. Cruisers
Folded us under their bow-waves, we bobbed up,
Happy enough. But the wind
Smartened against us, and the tide turned, roughening,
Dragged seaward. We rowed. We rowed. We
Saw we weren't going to make it. We turned,
Cutting downwind for the sand-bar, beached
And wondered what next. It was there
I found a horse-shoe crab's carapace, perfect,
No bigger than a bee, in honey-pale cellophane.
No way back. But big, good America found us.
A power-boat and a pilot of no problems.
He roped our boat to his stern and with all his family
Slammed back across the channel into the wind,
The spray scything upwards, our boat behind
Twisting across the wake-boil – a hectic
Four or five minutes and he cast us off
In the lee of the land, but a mile or more
From our dock. We toiled along inshore. We came
To a back-channel, under beach-house gardens – marsh grass,
Wild, original greenery of America,
Mud-slicks and fiddler-crab warrens, as we groped
Towards the harbour. Gloom-rich water. Something
Suggested easy plenty. We lowered baits,

And out of about six feet of water
Six or seven feet from land, we pulled up flounders
Big as big plates, till all our bait had gone.
After our wind-burned, head-glitter day of emptiness,
And the slogging row for our lives, and the rescue,
Suddenly out of water easy as oil
The sea piled our boat with its surplus. And the day
Curled out of brilliant, arduous morning,
Through wind-hammered perilous afternoon,
Salt-scoured, to a storm-gold evening, a luxury
Of rowing among the dream-yachts of the rich
Lolling at anchor off the play-world pier.

How tiny an adventure
To stay so monumental in our marriage,
A slight ordeal of all that might be,
And a small thrill-breath of what many live by,
And a small prize, a toy miniature
Of the life that might have bonded us
Into a single animal, a single soul –

It was a visit from the goddess, the beauty
Who was poetry's sister – she had come
To tell poetry she was spoiling us.
Poetry listened, maybe, but we heard nothing
And poetry did not tell us. And we
Only did what poetry told us to do.

Clive James

Holding Court

Retreating from the world, all I can do
Is build a new world, one demanding less
Acute assessments. Too deaf to keep pace
With conversation, I don't try to guess
At meanings, or unpack a stroke of wit,
But just send silent signals with my face
That claim I've not succumbed to loneliness
And might be ready to come in on cue.
People still turn towards me where I sit.

I used to notice everything, and spoke
A language full of details that I'd seen,
And people were amused; but now I see
Only a little way. What can they mean,
My phrases? They come drifting like the mist
I look through if someone appears to be
Smiling in my direction. Have they been?
This was the time when I most liked to smoke.
My watch-band feels too loose around my wrist.

My body, sensitive in every way
Save one, can still proceed from chair to chair,
But in my mind the fires are dying fast.
Breathe through a scarf. Steer clear of the cold air.
Think less of love and all that you have lost.
You have no future so forget the past.
Let this be no occasion for despair.
Cherish the prison of your waning day.
Remember liberty, and what it cost.

Be pleased that things are simple now, at least,
As certitude succeeds bewilderment.
The storm blew out and this is the dead calm.

The pain is going where the passion went.
Few things will move you now to lose your head
And you can cause, or be caused, little harm.
Tonight you leave your audience content:
You were the ghost they wanted at the feast,
Though none of them recalls a word you said.

Kathleen Jamie

Speirin

Binna feart, hinny,
yin day we'll gang thegither
tae thae stourie
blaebellwids,
and loss wirsels –

see, I'd raither
whummel a single oor
intae the blae o thae wee flo'ers
than live fur a' eternity
in some cauld hivvin.

Wheest, nou, till I spier o ye
will ye haud wi me?

Alan Jenkins

Effects

I held her hand, that was always scarred
From chopping, slicing, from the knives that lay in wait
In bowls of washing-up, that was raw,
The knuckles reddened, rough from scrubbing hard
At saucepan, frying pan, cup and plate
And giving love the only way she knew,
In each cheap cut of meat, in roast and stew,
Old-fashioned food she cooked and we ate;
And I saw that they had taken off her rings,
The rings she'd kept once in her dressing-table drawer
With faded snapshots, long-forgotten things
(Scent-sprays, tortoise-shell combs, a snap or two
From the time we took a holiday 'abroad')
But lately had never been without, as if
She wanted everyone to know she was his wife
Only now that he was dead. And her watch? –
Classic ladies' model, gold strap – it was gone,
And I'd never known her not have *that* on,
Not in all the years they sat together
Watching soaps and game shows I'd disdain
And not when my turn came to cook for her,
Chops or chicken portions, English, bland,
Familiar flavours she said she preferred
To whatever 'funny foreign stuff'
Young people seemed to eat these days, she'd heard;
Not all the weeks I didn't come, when she sat
Night after night and stared unseeing at
The television, at her inner weather,
Heaved herself upright, blinked and poured
Drink after drink, and gulped and stared – the scotch
That, when he was alive, she wouldn't touch,
That was her way to be with him again;
Not later in the psychiatric ward,

Where she blinked unseeing at the wall, the nurses
(Who would steal anything, she said), and dreamt
Of when she was a girl, of the time before
I was born, or grew up and learned contempt,
While the TV in the corner blared
To drown some 'poor soul's' moans and curses,
And she took her pills and blinked and stared
As the others shuffled round, and drooled, and swore…
But now she lay here, a thick rubber band
With her name on it in smudged black ink was all she wore
On the hand I held, a blotched and crinkled hand
Whose fingers couldn't clasp mine any more
Or falteringly wave, or fumble at my sleeve –
The last words she had said were *Please don't leave*
But of course I left; now I was back, though she
Could not know that, or turn her face to see
A nurse bring the little bag of her effects to me.

Linton Kwesi Johnson

Mi Revalueshanary Fren

mi revalueshanary fren is nat di same agen
yu know fram wen?
fram di masses shattah silence–
staat fi grumble
fram pawty paramoncy tek a tumble
fram Hungary to Poelan to Romania
fram di cozy kyawsl dem staat fi crumble
wen wi buck-up wananada in a reaznin
mi fren always en up pan di same ting
dis is di sang im love fi sing:

Kaydar[1]
e ad to go
Zhivkov[2]
e ad to go
Husak[3]
e ad to go
Honnicka[4]
e ad to go
Chowcheskhu[5]
e ad to go
jus like apartied
will av to go

Notes
1 Kadar – last communist leader of Hungary
2 Last communist leader of Bulgaria
3 Last communist leader of Czechoslovakia
4 Honecker – last communist leader of East Germany
5 Ceausescu – last communist leader of Romania

awhile agoh mi fren an mi woz taakin
soh mi seh to him:

wat a way di ert a run nowadays, man
it gettin aadah by di day
fi know whe yu stan
cauz wen yu tink yu deh pan salid dry lan
wen yu tek a stack yu fine yu inna quick-san
yu noh notice how di lanscape a shif
is like valcanoe andah it an notn cyaan stap it
cauz tings jusa bubble an a bwoil doun below
strata separate an refole
an wen yu tink yu reach di mountain tap
is a bran-new platow yu goh buck-up

mi revalueshanary fren shake him hed an him sigh
dis woz im reply:

Kaydar
e ad to go
Zhivkov
e ad to go
Husak
e ad to go
Honnicka
e ad to go
Chowcheskhu
e ad to go
jus like apartied
will av to go

well mi nevah did satisfy wid wat mi fren mek reply
an fi get a deepah meanin in di reaznin
mi seh to im:

well awrite
soh Garby gi di people dem glashnas
an it poze di Stallinist dem plenty prablem
soh Garby leggo peristrika pan dem
canfoundin bureacratic strategems
but wi haffi face up to di cowl facks
him also open up pandora's bax
yes, people powah jus a showah evry howah
an evrybady claim dem demacratic
but some a wolf an some a sheep
an dat is prablematic
noh tings like dat yu woulda call dialectic?

mi revalueshanary fren pauz awhile an him smile
den him look mi in mi eye an reply:

Kaydar
e ad to go
Zhivkov
e ad to go
Husak
e ad to go
Honnicka
e ad to go
Chowcheskhu
e ad to go
jus like apartied
will av to go

well mi coudn elabarate
plus it woz gettin kinda late
soh in spite a mi lack af andastandin
bout di meanin a di changes
in di east fi di wes, nondiles
an alldow mi av mi rezavaeshans
bout di cansiquenses an implicaeshans
espehshally fi black libahraeshan

to bring di reaznin to a canclueshan
I ad woz to agree wid mi fren
hopin dat wen wi meet up wance agen
wi coulda av a more fulah canvahsaeshan

soh mi seh to him, yu know wat?
him seh wat? mi seh:

Kaydar
e ad to go
Zhivkov
e ad to go
Husak
e ad to go
Honnicka
e ad to go
Chowcheskhu
e ad to go
jus like apartied
soon gaan

Jackie Kay

Late Love

How they strut about, people in love,
how tall they grow, pleased with themselves,
their hair, glossy, their skin shining.
They don't remember who they have been.

How filmic they are just for this time.
How important they've become – secret, above
the order of things, the dreary mundane.
Every church bell ringing, a fresh sign.

How dull the lot that are not in love.
Their clothes shabby, their skin lustreless;
how clueless they are, hair a mess; how they trudge
up and down streets in the rain,

remembering one kiss in a dark alley,
a touch in a changing-room, if lucky, a lovely wait
for the phone to ring, maybe, baby.
The past with its rush of velvet, its secret hush

already miles away, dimming now, in the late day.

Mimi Khalvati

The Swarm

Snow was literally swarming round the streetlamp like gnats.
The closer they came, the larger they grew, snow-gnats, snow-bees,

and in my snood, smoking in the snow, I watched them.
Everyone else was behind the door, I could hear their noise

which made the snow, the swarm, more silent. More welcome.
I could have watched for hours and seen nothing more than specks

against the light interrupting light and away from it, flying blind
but carrying light, specks becoming atoms. They flew too fast

to become snow itself, flying in a random panic, looming close
but disappearing, like flakes on the tongue, at the point of recognition.

They died as they landed, riding on their own melting as poems do
and in the morning there was nothing to be seen of them.

Instead, a streak of lemon, lemon honey, ringed the sky
but the cloud-lid never lifted, the weekend promised a blizzard.

I could have watched for hours and seen nothing more than I do now,
an image, metaphor, but not the blind imperative that drove them.

John Kinsella

The Hierarchy of Sheep – a report from my brother

1 *Rams*

To be lamb meat or castrated to wethers
or reign in longevity and fertility
and throw the shearer who can't afford
to hit back, golden balls hanging like trophies,
deep wrinkles genetically engineered
bringing the long merino wool as fine
as the buyer could want, as lambs
of an old ram with a kick so hard
that it takes a couple of roustabouts
to hold it down, will be as boisterous
and determined to take the world on –
'there is a lot of genetics in sheep,
even their temperament'.

A ram horns its way into the blue singlet
of a shearer and through to his belly,
coiled like the spiral matrix of hatred
recognising captivity – fly strike
thickening wool with goo and maggots,
possibly a rogue that's broken down fences,
furious amongst the ewes, savage to its fellows,
headbutting and cracking the competition –
the shearer wastes his enemy with a jet
of aero-start up the nostrils, abusing the farmer
for feeding the bastard lupins and lime
while he watches on nervously, fearing a vengeful shearer
as the feelers sense their way out of the sheath
of the ram's penis – cut by the handpiece
the ram is rendered 'useless',
unable to find the ewe's cunt.

2 *Ewes*

All cut by a shearer at one time or another –
sewn together with dental floss or wearing their scars
gracefully beneath the new season's haute-couture,
role play as if gender has meaning out there –
collectively warding a fox from the lambs.
Earlier the farmer assisted a birth
and then shot a mother polluted by stillbirth –
utilitarian in the way of things. Months back
he'd joked as rams were unleashed
into a ripe flock; up with the crack of dawn,
watching the weather, noticing the comings
and goings of birds. Now rain threatens
and older ewes kick like hell,
all of them full with young, milk veins
up and pumping hard to udders –
somewhere a nick with a blade has a vein
knotted off with needle and thread,
the myth declaring that another takes its place.
'Sometimes ewes get nervous and sensing
their humility is not hard. They get this manic shake
and tears fall from the corners of their eyes.'
A lamb drops in a catching pen.
A shearer aims a teat at his mate
and squirts a shot of milk into his ear.
The shed is full of swearing and laughter.

3 *Wethers*

Low maintenance power houses
scouring the goldfields for scant feed
their wool full of wool spiders, chewing
a shearer's singlet to extract salt
as the handpiece worms off a strip of flesh
and bleats come from somewhere deep
inside, wiry and up against it the farmer

keeping them on a slender thread
to boost the quality of wool – harsh
conditions producing fine strands.
A fly-struck wether with flesh
hanging in sheets and flies erupting
from its ribcage has a fly-killing
poison sprayed into its cavities –
but not even this and the remnants
of testosterone can keep it upright
and a short while later the dull thud
of a gun being fired somewhere outside
moves contrapuntally into the shed,
teasing the buzz of the plant, downtubes whirring,
handpieces snatched in and out of gear.
Even the dead added to the tally.

4 *Lambs*
The assault comes on strong: tailed,
castrated, ringed, earmarked, and mulesed.
Tails gas-axed off. Alive and highly strung
and either moving on to weaner
then hogget then ram, ewe, or wether,
or consumed while the flesh is tender.

August Kleinzahler

Epistle XXXIX

Aggrievius, how is it that I'm certain that you, no other,
will be the one to speak most eloquently at my memorial?
Because it is you, dear friend, who best husbanded
kind remarks of any sort, and, likewise, praise, in life,
the better that it might gush forth now in a single, extravagant go.
There you are, struggling, fighting back your grief. It's evident
to everyone on hand: the strangled, staccato bursts,
the troubled breathing. Hang in there, old son, you've rehearsed
too long and hard to get tangled up in sentiment now.
There, there, you're beginning to calm down. We're all relieved,
even me, and I'm dead. Behold, Aggrievius, in full sail,
canvas snapping in the wind as we approach his peroration.
It's true, you know, I really was a decent chap, underneath:
kind to dogs, shop clerks – and something of a wit, to boot.
You trot out a few of my *bons mots* to make that very point, suggesting
that my more fierce or pungent asides are better left shelved
for now. – *Ho, ho, ho*, the assembled murmur, demurely.
A few of the best were at your expense, but we'll let that go.
You would have filed in, the lot of you, to Biber's *Rosary Sonatas*,
the Crucifixion part, 'Agony in the Garden,' all that.
Hardly the soundtrack, one would have guessed, for an old, dead Jew.
Quite a few of these chicks on hand have it going on still, eh?
You'd really have to blow it big time not to get laid,
what with all the tears, perfume, black lace…Am I being awful?
Forgive me. But it is my party, after all. *After all*, after all.
I'd say, on balance, it was a very nice show. In fact,
I might as well have scripted it myself, perhaps with better pacing.
But I could not have improved upon your speech, Aggrievius, no.
It really is you, finally, who knew me best and loathed me most.

RF Langley

To a Nightingale

Nothing along the road. But
petals, maybe. Pink behind
and white inside. Nothing but
the coping of a bridge. Mutes
on the bricks, hard as putty,
then, in the sun, as metal.
Burls of *Grimmia*, hairy,
hoary, with their seed-capsules
uncurling. Red mites bowling
about on the baked lichen
and what look like casual
landings, striped flies, *Helina*,
Phaonia, could they be?
This month the lemon, I'll say
primrose-coloured, moths, which flinch
along the hedge then turn in
to hide, are Yellow Shells not
Shaded Broad-bars. Lines waver.
Camptogramma. Heat off the
road and the nick-nack of names.
Scotopteryx. Darkwing. The
flutter. Doubles and blurs the
margin. Fuscous and white. Stop
at nothing. To stop here at
nothing, as a chaffinch sings
interminably, all day.
A chiff-chaff. Purring of two
turtle doves. Voices, and some
vibrate with tenderness. I
say none of this for love. It
is anyone's giff-gaff. It
is anyone's quelque chose.
No business of mine. Mites which

ramble. Caterpillars which
curl up as question marks. Then
one note, five times, louder each
time, followed, after a fraught
pause, by a soft cuckle of
wet pebbles, which I could call
a glottal rattle. I am
empty, stopped at nothing, as
I wait for this song to shoot.
The road is rising as it
passes the apple tree and
makes its approach to the bridge.

James Lasdun

Stones

I'm trying to solve the problem of the paths
between the beds. A six-inch cover
of cedar chips that took a month to lay
rotted in two years and turned to weeds.
I scraped them up and carted them away,
then planted half a sack of clover seeds
for a 'living mulch'. I liked that: flowers
strewn along like stars, the cupid's bow
drawn on each leaf like thumbnail quartermoons,
its easy, springy give – until it spread
under the split trunks framing off each bed,
scribbling them over in its own
green graffiti…I ripped it out
and now I'm trying to set these paths in stone.
It isn't hard to find: the ground here's littered
with rough-cut slabs, some of them so vast
you'd think a race of giants must have lived here
building some bluestone Carnac or Stonehenge,
us their dwindled offspring, foraging
among their ruins…I scavenge
lesser pieces; pry them from the clutches
of tree-roots, lift them out of ditches,
filch them from our own stone wall
guiltily, though they're mine to take,
then wrestle them on board the two-wheeled dolly
and drag them up the driveway to the fence,
where, in a precarious waltz, I tip
and twist them backward, tilting all their weight
first on one corner, then the other
and dance them slowly through the garden gate.
The hard part's next, piecing them together;
a matter of blind luck and infinite pains:
one eye open for the god-given fit –

this stone's jagged key to that one's lock –
the other quietly gauging how to fudge it:
split the difference on angles, cram the gaps
with stone-dust filler; hoping what the rains
don't wash away, the frost will pack and harden…
A chipmunk blinks and watches from his rock,
wondering if I've lost my mind perhaps.
Perhaps I have; out here every day,
cultivating – no, not even that;
tending the inverse spaces of my garden
(it's like a blueprint now, for Bluebeard's castle),
while outside, by degrees, the planet slips
– a locking piece – into apocalypse,
but somehow I can't tear myself away:
I like the drudgery; I seem to revel
in pitting myself against the sheer
recalcitrance of the stones; using
their awkwardness – each cupped or bulging face,
every cockeyed bevel and crooked curve,
each quirk of outline (this one a cracked lyre,
that one more like a severed head) –
to send a flickering pulse along the border
so that it seems to ripple round each bed
with an unstonelike, liquid grace:
'the best stones in the best possible order'
or some such half-remembered rule in mind,
as if it mattered, making some old stones
say or be anything but stone, stone, stone;
as if these paths might serve some purpose
aside from making nothing happen; as if
their lapidary line might lead me somewhere –
inward, onward, upward, anywhere
other than merely back where I began,
wondering where I've been, and what I've done.

Gwyneth Lewis

Mother Tongue

'I started to translate in seventy-three
in the schoolyard. For a bit of fun
to begin with – the occasional "fuck"
for the bite of another language's smoke
at the back of my throat, its bitter chemicals.
Soon I was hooked on whole sentences
behind the shed, and lessons in Welsh
seemed very boring. I started on print,
Jeeves & Wooster, Dick Francis, James Bond,
in Welsh covers. That worked for a while
until Mam discovered Jean Plaidy inside
a Welsh concordance one Sunday night.
There were ructions: a language, she screamed,
should be for a lifetime. Too late for me.
Soon I was snorting Simenon
and Flaubert. Had to read much more
for any effect. One night I OD'd
after reading far too much Proust.
I came to, but it scared me. For a while
I went Welsh-only but it was bland
and my taste was changing. Before too long
I was back on translating, found that three
languages weren't enough. The "ch"
in German was easy, Rilke a buzz...
For a language fetishist like me
sex is part of the problem. Umlauts make me sweat,
so I need a multilingual man
but they're rare in West Wales and tend to be
married already. If only I'd kept
myself much purer, with simpler tastes,
the Welsh might be living...

                     Detective, you speak
Russian, I hear, and Japanese.
Could you whisper some softly?
I'm begging you. Please…'

Michael Longley

Cloudberries

You give me cloudberry jam from Lapland,
Bog amber, snow-line titbits, scrumptious
Cloudberries sweetened slowly by the cold,
And costly enough for cloudberry wars
(Diplomatic wars, my dear).
                          Imagine us
Among the harvesters, keeping our distance
In sphagnum fields on the longest day
When dawn and dusk like frustrated lovers
Can kiss, legend has it, once a year. Ah,
Kisses at our age, cloudberry kisses.

Hannah Lowe

Dance Class

The best girls posed like poodles at a show
and Betty Finch, in lemon gauze and wrinkles,
swept her wooden cane along the rows
to lock our knees in place and turn our ankles.
I was a scandal in that class, big-footed
giant in lycra, joker in my tap shoes,
slapping on the off-beat while a hundred
tappers hit the wood. I missed the cues
each time. After, in the foyer, dad,
a black man, stood among the Essex mothers
clad in leopard skin. He'd shake his keys
and scan the bloom of dancers where I hid
and whispered to another ballerina
he's the cab my mother sends for me.

Roddy Lumsden

Yeah Yeah Yeah

No matter what you did to her, she said,
There's times, she said, she misses you, your face
Will pucker in her dream, and times the bed's
Too big. Stray hairs will surface in a place
You used to leave your shoes. A certain phrase,
Some old song on the radio, a joke
You had to be there for, she said, some days
It really gets to her; the way you smoked
Or held a cup, or her, and how you woke
Up crying in the night sometimes, the way
She'd stroke and hush you back, and how you broke
Her still. All this she told me yesterday,
Then she rolled over, laughed, began to do
To me what she so rarely did with you.

Derek Mahon

Death in Bangor

We stand — not many of us — in a new cemetery
on a cold hillside in the north of Co. Down
staring at an open grave or out to sea,
the lough half-hidden by great drifts of rain.
Only a few months since you were snug at home
in a bungalow glow, keeping provincial time
in the chimney corner, *News-Letter* and *Woman's Own*
on your knee, wool-gathering by Plato's firelight,
a grudging flicker of flame on anthracite.
Inactive since your husband died, your chief
concern the 'appearances' that ruled your life
in a neighbourhood of bay windows and stiff
gardens shivering in the salt sea air,
the rising-sun motif on door and gate,
you knew the secret history of needlework,
bread-bin and laundry basket awash with light,
the straight-backed chairs, the madly chiming clock.
The figure in the *Republic* returns to the cave,
a Dutch interior where cloud-shadows move,
to examine the intimate spaces, chest and drawer,
the lavender in the linen, the savings book,
the kitchen table silent with nobody there.
Shall we say the patience of an angel? No,
not unless angels be thought anxious too
and God knows you had reason to be; for yours
was an anxious time of nylon and bakelite,
market-driven hysteria on every fretwork radio,
your frantic kitsch decor designed for you
by thick industrialists and twisted ministers
('Nature's a bad example to simple folk'); and yet
with your wise monkeys and euphemistic 'Dresden' figurines,
your junk chinoiserie and coy pastoral scenes,

you too were a kind of artist, a rage-for-order freak
setting against a man's aesthetic of cars and golf
your ornaments and other breakable stuff.
Visible from your window the sixth-century
abbey church of Colum and Malachi,
'light of the world' once in the monastic ages,
home of antiphonary and the radiant pages
of shining scripture; though you had your own
idea of the beautiful, not unrelated to Tolstoy
but formed in a tough city of ships and linen,
Harland & Wolff, Mackie's, Gallaher's, Lyle & Kinahan
and your own York St. Flax Spinning Co. Ltd.,
where you worked with a thousand others before the war;
of trams and shopping arcades, dance-hall and 'milk bar',
cold picnics at Whitehead and Donaghadee,
of Henry Joy McCracken and Wolfe Tone,
a glimmer of hope indefinitely postponed,
daft musicals at the Curzon and the Savoy;
later, a bombing raid glimpsed from your bedroom window,
utility clothing, US armoured divisions here,
the dwindling industries. (Where now the great
liners that raised their bows at the end of the street?
Ophidian shapes among the chandeliers,
wood-boring organisms at the swirling stairs.)
Beneath a Castilian sky, at a great mystic's rococo tomb,
I thought of the plain Protestant fatalism of home.
Remember 1690; prepare to meet thy God.
I grew up among washing-lines and grey skies,
pictures of Brookeborough on the gable-ends,
revolvers, RUC, B-Specials, law-'n'-order,
a hum of drums above the summer glens
echoing like *Götterdämmerung* over lough water
in a violent post-industrial sunset blaze
while you innocently hummed 'South of the Border',
'On a Slow Boat to China', 'Beyond the Blue Horizon'.

...Little soul, the body's guest and companion,
this is a cold epitaph from your only son,
the wish genuine if the tone ambiguous.
Oh, I can love you now that you're dead and gone
to the many mansions in your mother's house.
All artifice stripped away, we give you back to nature
but something of you, perhaps the incurable ache
of art, goes with me as I travel south
past misty drumlins, shining lanes to the shore,
above the Mournes a final helicopter,
sun-showers and rainbows all the way through Louth,
cottages buried deep in ivy and rhododendron,
ranch houses, dusty palms, blue skies of the republic...

Glyn Maxwell

The Byelaws

Never have met me, know me well,
tell all the world there was little to tell,
say I was heavenly, say I was hell,
harry me over the blasted moors
        but come my way, go yours.

Never have touched me, take me apart,
trundle me through my town in a cart,
figure me out with the aid of a chart,
finally add to the feeble applause
        and come my way, go yours.

Never have read me, look at me now,
get why I'm doing it, don't get how,
other way round, have a rest, have a row,
have skirmishes with me, have wars,
        O come my way, go yours.

Never have left me, never come back,
mourn me in miniskirts, date me in black,
undress as I dress, when I unpack pack
yet pause for eternity on all fours
        to come my way, go yours.

Never have met me, never do,
never be mine, never even be you,
approach from a point it's impossible to
at a time you don't have, and by these byelaws
        come my way, go yours.

Roger McGough

The Way Things Are

No, the candle is not crying, it cannot feel pain.
Even telescopes, like the rest of us, grow bored.
Bubblegum will not make the hair soft and shiny.
The duller the imagination, the faster the car,
I am your father and this is the way things are.

When the sky is looking the other way,
do not enter the forest. No, the wind
is not caused by the rushing of clouds.
An excuse is as good a reason as any.
A lighthouse, launched, will not go far,
I am your father and this is the way things are.

No, old people do not walk slowly
because they have plenty of time.
Gardening books when buried will not flower.
Though lightly worn, a crown may leave a scar,
I am your father and this is the way things are.

No, the red woolly hat has not been
put on the railing to keep it warm.
When one glove is missing, both are lost.
Today's craft fair is tomorrow's car boot sale.
The guitarist gently weeps, not the guitar,
I am your father and this is the way things are.

Pebbles work best without batteries.
The deckchair will fail as a unit of currency.
Even though your shadow is shortening
it does not mean you are growing smaller.
Moonbeams sadly, will not survive in a jar,
I am your father and this is the way things are.

For centuries the bullet remained quietly confident
that the gun would be invented.
A drowning Dadaist will not appreciate
the concrete lifebelt.
No guarantee my last goodbye is au revoir,
I am your father and this is the way things are.

Do not become a prison-officer unless you know
what you're letting someone else in for.
The thrill of being a shower curtain will soon pall.
No trusting hand awaits the falling star,
I am your father, and I am sorry,
but this is the way things are.

Jamie McKendrick

Home Thoughts

The airmail from India, a weatherbeaten blue,
with wax marks from the candle you had used
to write by reached me. You write that reach
is what travellers there do rather than arrive
being more respectful to the gods of place.
For years your letters from around the world
have kept on reaching me wherever
I'm hunched beside an atlas and a lamp.
When you last saw me I was living in a room
across the road from but a floor below
the room we used to share ten years ago.
Only kindness stopped you saying
it took me quite some time to cross that road;
and looking from my window I expect to see
myself looking out to where in ten years time
I'll be looking back again to see...the last things
you mention are the Parsee towers of silence
where the dead are left for vultures to attend.
I warm to that. It sort of brings things home.

Kei Miller

in which the cartographer asks for directions

Sometimes the cartographer gets frustrated when he asks an I-formant how to get to such and such a place, and the I-formant might say something like –

> Awrite, you know the big white house at the bottom of
> Clover Hill with all the windows dem board up, and
> with a high shingle roof that look almost like a church?

Yes, the cartographer says.

> And in front the house you always see a ole woman,
> only three teeth in her mouth, and she out there selling
> pepper shrimp in a school chair with a umbrella tie to it.
> And beside her she always have two mongrel dog and
> one of them is white and the nedda one is brown?

Yes, I know exactly where you mean, the cartographer says.

> And in the yard there is a big guinnep tree that hang
> right out to the road, so school pickney always stop
> there to buy shrimp and eat free guinnep?

Yes, yes, the cartographer insists. I know it.

> Good, says the I-formant. Cause you mustn' go there.

Sinéad Morrissey

The Coal Jetty

Twice a day,
    whether I'm lucky enough
        to catch it or not,

the sea slides out
    as far as it can go
        and the shore coughs up

its crockery: rocks,
    mussel banks, beach glass,
        the horizontal chimney stacks

of sewer pipes,
    crab shells, bike spokes.
        As though a floating house

fell out of the clouds
    as it passed
        the city limits,

Belfast bricks, the kind
    that also built the factories
        and the gasworks,

litter the beach.
    Most of the landing jetty
        for coal's been washed

away by storms; what stands—
    a section of platform
        with sky on either side—

is home now to guillemots
    and cormorants
        who call up

the ghosts of nineteenth-
    century hauliers
        with their blackened

beaks and wings.
    At the lowest ebb,
        even the scum at the rim

of the waves
    can't reach it.
        We've been down here

before, after dinner,
    picking our way
        over mudflats and jellyfish

to the five spiked
    hallways underneath,
        spanned like a viaduct.

There's the stink
    of rust and salt,
        of cooped-up

water just released
    to its wider element.
        What's left is dark and quiet—

barnacles, bladderwrack,
   brick—but book-ended
      by light,

as when Dorothy
   opens her dull
      cabin door

and what happens outside is Technicolor.

Paul Muldoon

Wire

As I roved out this morning at daybreak
I took a shortcut
through the pine forest, following the high-tension wires
past the timberline
till I stumbled upon a makeshift hide or shooting box
from which a command wire seemed to run

intermittently along the ski run
or firebreak.
I glanced into the hideout. A school lunchbox.
A pear so recently cut
I thought of Ceylon. A can of Valvoline.
Crocodile clips. Sri Lanka, I mean. A hank of wire

that might come in handy if ever I'd want to hot-wire
a motor and make a run
for the border. From just beyond my line
of vision I glimpsed something, or someone, break
cover for an instant. A shaved head, maybe, or a crew cut.
Jumping up like a jack-in-the-box

before ducking back down. Then a distant raking through the gearbox
of a truck suddenly gone haywire
on this hillside of hillsides in Connecticut
brought back some truck on a bomb run,
brought back so much with which I'd hoped to break—
the hard line

yet again refusing to toe the line,
the bullet and the ballot box,
the joyride, the jail break,
Janet endlessly singing "The Men Behind the Wire",
the endless rerun
of Smithfield, La Mon, Enniskillen, of bodies cut

to ribbons as I heard the truck engine cut
and, you might have read as much between the lines,
ducked down here myself behind the hide. As if I myself were on
    the run.
The truck driver handing a box
cutter, I'm sure, to the bald guy. A pair of real live wires.
I've listened to them all day now, torn between making a break

for it and their talk of the long run, the short term, of boxing clever,
fish or cut bait, make or break,
the end of the line, right down to the wire.

Les Murray

The Shield-Scales of Heraldry

Surmounting my government's high evasions
stands a barbecue of crosses and birds
tended by a kangaroo and emu
but in our courts, above the judge,
a lion and a unicorn still keep
their smaller offspring, plus a harp,
in an open prison looped with mottoes.

Coats of arms, plaster Rorschach blots,
crowned stone moths, they encrust Europe.
As God was dismissed from churches
they fluttered in and cling to the walls,
abstract comic-pages held by scrolled beasts,
or wear on the flagstones underfoot.
They pertain to an earlier Antichrist,

the one before police. Mafiose citadels
made them, states of one attended family
islanded in furrows. The oldest
are the simplest. A cross, some coins,
a stripe, a roof tree, a spur rowel,
bowstaves, a hollow-gutted lion,
and all in lucid target colours.

Under tinned heads with reveries tied on,
shields are quartered and cubed by marriage
till they are sacred campaign maps
or anatomy inside dissected mantling,
glyphs minutely clear through their one
rule, that colour must abut either
gold or silver, the non-weapon metals.

The New World doesn't blazon well –
the new world ran away from blazonry
or was sent away in chains by it –
but exceptions shine: the spread eagle
with the fireworks display on its belly
and in the thinks-balloon above its head.
And when as a half-autistic

kid in scrub paddocks vert and or
I grooved on the cloisons of pedigree
it was a vivid writing of system
that hypnotised me, beyond the obvious
euphemism of force. It was eight hundred
years of cubist art and Europe's dreamings:
the Cup, the Rose, the Ship, the Antlers.

High courage, bestial snobbery,
neither now merits ungrace from us.
They could no longer hang me,
throttling, for a rabbit sejant.
Like everyone, I would now be lord
or lady myself, and pardon me
or myself loose the coronet-necked hounds.

Now we face new people who share
attitudes only with each other,
withholding all fellowship with us,
all genial laughter. Reverse nobles
who twist us into Gorgon shapes
of an anti-heraldry, inside
their journals and never-lowered shields.

Daljit Nagra

Look We Have Coming to Dover!

> *'So various, so beautiful, so new...'*
> Matthew Arnold, 'Dover Beach'

Stowed in the sea to invade
the alfresco lash of a diesel-breeze
ratcheting speed into the tide, brunt with
gobfuls of surf phlegmed by cushy come-and-go
tourists prow'd on the cruisers, lording the ministered waves.

Seagull and shoal life
vexing their blarnies upon our huddled
camouflage past the vast crumble of scummed
cliffs, scramming on mulch as thunder unbladders
yobbish rain and wind on our escape hutched in a Bedford van.

Seasons or years we reap
inland, unclocked by the national eye
or stabs in the back, teemed for breathing
sweeps of grass through the whistling asthma of parks,
burdened, ennobled – poling sparks across pylon and pylon.

Swarms of us, grafting in
the black within shot of the moon's
spotlight, banking on the miracle of sun –
span its rainbow, passport us to life. Only then
can it be human to hoick ourselves, bare-faced for the clear.

Imagine my love and I,
our sundry others, Blair'd in the cash
of our beeswax'd cars, our crash clothes, free,
we raise our charged glasses over unparasol'd tables
East, babbling our lingoes, flecked by the chalk of Britannia!

Sean O'Brien

The Politics of

When I walk by your house, I spit.
That's not true. I *intend* to.
When you're at breakfast with the *Daily Mail*
Remember me. I'm here about this time,
Disabled by restraint and staring.
But I do not send the bag of excrement,
Decapitate your dog at night,
Or press you to a glass of Paraquat,
Or hang you by your bollocks from a tree,
Still less conceal the small home-made device
Which blows your head off, do I, prat?
I think you'll have to grant me that,
Because I haven't. But I might.
If I were you, I'd be afraid of me.

Alice Oswald

A Greyhound in the Evening after a Long Day of Rain

Two black critical matching crows,
calling a ricochet, eating its answer,

dipped
    home

and a minute later
the ground was a wave and the sky wouldn't float.

*

With a task and a rake,
with a clay-slow boot and a yellow mack,
I bolted for shelter under the black strake dripping of timber,

summer of rain, summer of green rain
coming everywhere all day down
through a hole in my foot.

*

Listen Listen Listen Listen

*

They are returning to the rain's den,
the grey folk, rolling up their veils,
taking the steel taps out of their tips and heels.

Grass lifts, hedge breathes,
rose shakes its hair,
birds bring out all their washed songs,
puddles like long knives flash on the roads.

*

And evening is come with a late sun unloading a silence,
tiny begin-agains dancing on the night's edge.

But what I want to know is
whose is the great grey wicker-limbed hound,
like a stepping on coal, going softly away…

Don Paterson

Nil Nil

> '*Just as any truly accurate representation of a particular
> geography can only exist on a scale of 1:1 (imagine the vast,
> rustling map of Burgundy, say, settling over it like a freshly-
> starched sheet!) so it is with all our abandoned histories,
> those ignoble lines of succession that end in neither triumph
> nor disaster, but merely plunge on into deeper and deeper
> obscurity; only in the infinite ghost-libraries of the imagina-
> tion – their only possible analogue – can their ends be
> pursued, the dull and terrible facts finally authenticated.*'
>
> François Aussemain, *Pensées*

From the top, then, the zenith, the silent footage:
McGrandle, majestic in ankle-length shorts,
his golden hair shorn to an open book, sprinting
the length of the park for the long hoick forward,
his balletic toe-poke nearly bursting the roof
of the net; a shaky pan to the Erskine St End
where a plague of grey bonnets falls out of the clouds.
But ours is a game of two halves, and this game
the semi they went on to lose; from here
it's all down, from the First to the foot of the Second,
McGrandle, Visocchi and Spankie detaching
like bubbles to speed the descent into pitch-sharing,
pay-cuts, pawned silver, the Highland Division,
the absolute sitters ballooned over open goals,
the dismal nutmegs, the scores so obscene
no respectable journal will print them; though one day
Farquhar's spectacular bicycle-kick
will earn him a name-check in Monday's obituaries.
Besides the one setback – the spell of giant-killing
in the Cup (Lochee Violet, then Aberdeen Bon Accord,
the deadlock with Lochee Harp finally broken
by Farquhar's own-goal in the replay)

nothing inhibits the fifty-year slide
into Sunday League, big tartan flasks,
open hatchbacks parked squint behind goal-nets,
the half-time satsuma, the dog on the pitch,
then the Boy's Club, sponsored by Skelly Assurance,
then Skelly Dry Cleaners, then nobody;
stud-harrowed pitches with one-in-five inclines,
grim fathers and perverts with Old English Sheepdogs
lining the touch, moaning softly.
Now the unrefereed thirty-a-sides,
terrified fat boys with callipers minding
four jackets on infinite, notional fields;
ten years of dwindling, half-hearted kickabouts
leaves two little boys – Alastair Watt,
who answers to 'Forty', and wee Horace Madden,
so smelly the air seems to quiver above him –
playing desperate two-touch with a bald tennis ball
in the hour before lighting-up time.
Alastair cheats, and goes off with the ball
leaving wee Horace to hack up a stone
and dribble it home in the rain;
past the stopped swings, the dead shanty-town
of allotments, the black shell of Skelly Dry Cleaners
and into his cul-de-sac, where, accidentally,
he neatly back-heels it straight into the gutter
then tries to swank off like he meant it.

Unknown to him, it is all that remains
of a lone fighter-pilot, who, returning at dawn
to find Leuchars was not where he'd left it,
took time out to watch the Sidlaws unsheathed
from their great black tarpaulin, the haar burn off Tayport
and Venus melt into Carnoustie, igniting
the shoreline; no wind, not a cloud in the sky
and no one around to admire the discretion
of his unscheduled exit: the engine plopped out
and would not re-engage, sending him silently

twirling away like an ash-key,
his attempt to bail out only partly successful,
yesterday having been April the 1st –
the ripcord unleashing a flurry of socks
like a sackful of doves rendered up to the heavens
in private irenicon. He caught up with the plane
on the ground, just at the instant the tank blew
and made nothing of him, save for his fillings,
his tackets, his lucky half-crown and his gallstone,
now anchored between the steel bars of a stank
that looks to be biting the bullet on this one.

In short, this is where you get off, reader;
I'll continue alone, on foot, in the failing light
following the trail as it steadily fades
into road-repairs, birdsong, the weather, nirvana,
the plot thinning down to a point so refined
not even the angels could dance on it. Goodbye.

Clare Pollard

Thinking of England

> '*And let the lesson to be – to be yersel's,*
> *Ye needna fash gin it's to be ocht else.*
> *To be yersel's – and to mak' that worth bein'...*'
>
> Hugh MacDiarmid,
'A Drunk Man Looks at the Thistle'

> ' *Let me take you on a journey to a foreign land...*'
>
> William Hague

I

Dusk-light; the news tells of another train derailed,
and shoppers buying up the shops, and livestock
being herded to the chop – their chops unfit to eat –
and politicians once more putting foot to mouth.
Through my east-end window –

                      over the tangled tree,
the council houses: some sardined with children,
catering-sized gallon tubs of cooking oil empty beside their bins;
some sheltering one of the three million children still in poverty;
some sold to Thatcher's fortunate –
now worth hundreds of thousands, more,
with rents devised to make even the well-off poor –
over the kids and dogs on a hanky of grass,
the burnt-out car, the hush-hush trendy warehouse bar,
ISLAM UNITE scrawled on a wall –

a man's voice trails its skittering wail across the sky,
and all around me people are preparing to pray
to a God to whom I am one of the damned.

And what did our great-grandmothers taste?
Perhaps pie and mash and jellied eels, or hash, pease pudding,
cobbler, cottage pie,
                              pasties and pickled eggs.
When I was small there was still Spam and jellied ham –
semolina, parkin, treacle tart.
Why have we not stood with our mothers,
floured and flushed beside the oven door,
watching our first Yorkshire puddings:
how their globed bellies swell?
Why was this not passed daughter to daughter?
When did the passing stop?
When did we choose to steal instead
from the daughters of all those we have hated or hurt:
gnocchi, noodles, couscous, naan, falafel, jerk?
For dinner I have chicken dupiaza from a foil tray –
how fitting England's national dish is not homemade but takeaway.
Through thrift – the rent is due – I boil my own rice up,
long-grain American.

III

You're so fortunate, they would exclaim, as I took photographs
of them beside King's Chapel, or of willows washing
their hair in the Cam, *to have all of this history around you.*

England's history is medieval pogroms;
it is Elizabeth, her skin a crust of Dover-white,
loosing galleons to pillage fruits, tobacco, men.
The bulging-eyed thieves swinging to the crowd's delight
metres from Shakespeare's Globe;
                                        stripping the churches;
Becket bleeding buckets on the floor;
and work-houses for the poor,
and the slave-trade; and raping the wife –

lie back and think of…crinolines, Crimea.
Missionaries hacking their one true path through the jungle.
Winston swearing: *We will fight them on the beaches!*

These people held the cargo of my genes within their blood.
Not all were good.
                    But how can I be held up as accountable?
And yet, all of the good they earned, and blessed me with
brings with it blame. Today I filled a form in –
ticked *White British* with a cringe of shame.

I am educated, middle-class, housed, well.
I am fat and rich on history's hell.

  IV

I remember bracken, and heather, and a gusty, gutsy
wind, and a plastic tub of windberries that filled
and emptied, its ink writing a whodunit on my face.

I remember Southport, where granny said fine ladies had once
gone to purchase linens, and the best. Catching the miniature
train down to Happy-Land, and my name in wet sand,

and my grandfather towelling the sand off my legs,
and then our picnic in the car – tinned salmon sandwiches,
a flask of tea, crosswords. A Penguin biscuit.

I remember sitting in an American bar having to squint
to read about abortion laws by the dim candlelight,
and sipping my six-dollar Cosmopolitan – with a dollar tip –

and thinking of our local; its open fire, the rain
on its windows, and you in it. Maybe on a Sunday
after a walk on the heath, and lamb with mint sauce,

and thinking how I never could leave.

V

Just finishing off the curry, when the football starts.
An England game. Satellites are readying themselves
to bounce the match around the globe,
and prove that we are not the power we were.

The crowd belts out 'God Save the Queen',
though they do not believe in God or Queen;
their strips red, white and blue –
two of these being borrowed hues; loaned colours we use
to drown out the white noise of ourselves.
We are the whitest of the white:
                                     once this meant *right* –
Christ's holy light; the opposite of night, or black –
but now it only points to lack, the blank of who we are.

Who ever celebrates St George's Day?
And did you hear the one about the Englishman…?

A friend of mine at home's a Bolton Wanderers fan:
they chant *White Army*.

VI

And then the news again, at ten –
sometimes it makes you want to pack and leave it all:

the floods, the fuel, the teacher shortage in the schools,
the bombing of Iraq, the heart attacks, long working hours
and little sex, racist police, cigarette tax, grants all axed,
three million children still in poverty,
the burnt out car, the takeaway,
the headlines about Krauts, the lager louts,
the wobbly bridge they built, the colonial guilt,
the needless pain, the rain, the rain,

the pogroms, the pink globe, the tangled tree,
the Raj, the rape, the linens,
all the endless fucking cups of tea...

but everyone speaks English now,

and sometimes, a voice trails its skittering wail across the sky,
and I feel not just gratitude, but pride.

Peter Porter

Last Words

In the beginning was the Word,
Not just the word of God but sounds
Where Truth was clarified or blurred.
Then Rhyme and Rhythm did the rounds
And justified their jumps and joins
By glueing up our lips and loins.

Once words had freshness on their breath.
The Poet who saw first that Death
Has only one true rhyme was made
The Leader of the Boys' Brigade.
Dead languages can scan and rhyme
Like birthday cards and *Lilac Time*.

And you can carve words on a slab
Or tow them through the air by plane,
Tattoo them with a painful jab
Or hang them in a window pane.
Unlike our bodies which decay,
Words, first and last, have come to stay.

Sheenagh Pugh

Envying Owen Beattie

To have stood on the Arctic island
by the graves where Franklin's men
buried their shipmates: good enough.

To hack through the permafrost
to the coffin, its loving plaque
cut from a tin can: better.

And freeing the lid; seeing
the young sailor cocooned in ice,
asleep in his glass case.

Then melting it so gently, inch
by inch, a hundred years
and more falling away, all the distance

of death a soft hiss of steam
on the air, till at last they cupped
two feet, bare and perfect,

in their hands, and choked up,
because it was any feet
poking out of the bedclothes.

And when the calm, pinched
twenty-year-old face
came free, and he lay there,

five foot four of authentic
Victorian adventurer, tuberculous,
malnourished: John Torrington

the stoker, who came so far
in the cold, and someone whispered:
It's like he's unconscious.

Then Beattie stooped; lifted him
out of bed, the six stone
limp in his arms, and the head lolled

and rested on his shoulder,
and he felt the rush
that reckless trust sends

through parents and lovers. To have him
like that; the frail, diseased
little time-traveller;

to feel the lashes prickle
your cheek; to be that close
to the parted lips:

you would know all the fairy-tales
spoke true: how could you not try
to wake him with a kiss?

Claudia Rankine

The new therapist specializes...

The new therapist specializes in trauma counseling. You have only ever spoken on the phone. Her house has a side gate that leads to a back entrance she uses for patients. You walk down a path bordered on both sides with deer grass and rosemary to the gate, which turns out to be locked.

At the front door the bell is a small round disc that you press firmly. When the door finally opens, the woman standing there yells, at the top of her lungs, Get away from my house! What are you doing in my yard?

It's as if a wounded Doberman pinscher or a German shepherd has gained the power of speech. And though you back up a few steps, you manage to tell her you have an appointment. You have an appointment? she spits back. Then she pauses. Everything pauses. Oh, she says, followed by, oh, yes, that's right. I am sorry.

I am so sorry, so, so sorry.

Denise Riley

Listening for lost people

Still looking for lost people – look unrelentingly.
'They died' is not an utterance in the syntax of life
where they belonged, no *belong* – reanimate them
not minding if the still living turn away, casually.
Winds ruck up its skin so the sea tilts from red-blue
to blue-red: into the puckering water go his ashes
who was steadier than these elements. Thickness
of some surviving thing that sits there, bland. Its
owner's gone nor does the idiot howl – while I'm
unquiet as a talkative ear. Spring heat, a cherry
tree's fresh bronze leaves fan out and gleam – to
converse with shades, yourself become a shadow.
The souls of the dead are the spirit of language:
you hear them alight inside that spoken thought.

Michael Symmons Roberts

Pika

Elusive, witnessed first on paper,
then in deserts, then one whole city.
Those on the outskirts called it
pikadon: flash-boom in Japanese.
Those who saw it closer shortened it
to *pika*: a flash without a voice.
Survivors said it entered them
through eyes, then mapped them
in an instant – silver and alive.
After that it went to one more city,
then back to sands and seas.

New Year's Day, Hiroshima, 1945:
outlandish snowfall for a warm
delta city. Seven great rivers,
seven dark threads in the blanket.
Bridges fill with marvellers.
Believers in ill omens keep
their mouths shut, for fear
of *tonarigumi*: keepers of morale.
Come summer everyone would know
that *pika* had prepared its way
with ice and painless beauty.

Robin Robertson

At Roane Head

for John Burnside

You'd know her house by the drawn blinds –
by the cormorants pitched on the boundary wall,
the black crosses of their wings hung out to dry.
You'd tell it by the quicken and the pine that hid it
from the sea and from the brief light of the sun,
and by Aonghas the collie, lying at the door
where he died: a rack of bones like a sprung trap.

A fork of barnacle geese came over, with that slow
squeak of rusty saws. The bitter sea's complaining pull
and roll; a whicker of pigeons, lifting in the wood.

She'd had four sons, I knew that well enough,
and each one wrong. All born blind, they say,
slack-jawed and simple, web-footed,
rickety as sticks. Beautiful faces, I'm told,
though blank as air.
Someone saw them once, outside, hirpling
down to the shore, chittering like rats,
and said they were fine swimmers,
but I would have guessed at that.

Her husband left her: said
they couldn't be his, they were more
fish than human,
said they were beglamoured,
and searched their skin for the showing marks.

For years she tended each difficult flame:
their tight, flickering bodies.
Each night she closed
the scales of their eyes to smoor the fire.

Until he came again,
that last time,
thick with drink, saying
he'd had enough of this,
all this witchery,
and made them stand
in a row by their beds,
twitching. Their hands
flapped; herring-eyes
rolled in their heads.
He went along the line
relaxing them
one after another
with a small knife.

They say she goes out every night to lay
blankets on the graves to keep them warm.
It would put the heart across you, all that grief.

There was an otter worrying in the leaves, a heron
loping slow over the water when I came
at scraich of day, back to her door.

She'd hung four stones in a necklace, wore
four rings on the hand that led me past the room
with four small candles burning
which she called 'the room of rain'.
Milky smoke poured up from the grate
like a waterfall in reverse
and she said my name,
and it was the only thing
and the last thing that she said.

She gave me a skylark's egg in a bed of frost;
gave me twists of my four sons' hair; gave me
her husband's head in a wooden box.
Then she gave me the sealskin, and I put it on.

Jacob Sam-La Rose

After Lazerdrome, McDonalds, Peckham Rye

*'What's clear, now, is / that there was music, that it's lasted, that it /
doesn't matter whether a player played it, / or whether it just played itself,
that it still is / playing, / that at least two gods exist…'*
Abdulah Sidran, 'A Dispute About God'

where I say goodbye to south-east London for the next 3 years
a gaggle of us   still damp   spilling in from the night before

early flock for a Sunday   six or seven A.M.   sleepless
drowning in light and all this quiet   after all that sweat
and darkness   all that flighty noise

this is the year one of the guys says music is the one thing
that won't ever let him down   that music is his religion

the year we're stopped and searched because we
fit the description   the year jungle music passes
out of fashion   stripped down

to naked beat and bass   and we club together   to dance
alone   in the dark   let the music play us   meat and bone

let music fill the empty spaces   rhythm in wads and scads
scattershot   crashing   wall to wall   to be baptised
by filtered drums   pressed snares and swollen b-lines

be baptised by city songs   urban hymns   seamless
sound   a brimming sea of sound   poured out

from towering speaker stacks   this is the year we stand
close enough   to feel the music   rise   its wing-beats
on our faces   drawing salt from our skin   released

then morning   small fries and a strawberry milkshake
counting coins for the cab back   sitting around a table

slouching in moulded seats   drowning in silence
light-headed   leavened   waiting
for the right moment to move

awake for too long   ears
still ringing   drum-drunk

eyes still adjusting to the light
a weight coming down

Ann Sansom

Voice

Call, by all means, but just once
don't use the *broken heart again* voice;
the *I'm sick to death of life and women
and romance* voice *but with a little help
I'll try to struggle on* voice

Spare me the promise and the curse
voice, the ansafoney *Call me, please
when you get in* voice, the *nobody knows
the trouble I've seen* voice; the *I'd value
your advice* voice.

I want the how it was voice;
the *call me irresponsible but aren't I nice* voice;
the *such a bastard but I warn them in advance* voice.
The *We all have weaknesses
and mine is being wicked* voice

the *life's short and wasting time's
the only vice* voice, the *stay in touch,
but out of reach* voice. I want to hear
the *things it's better not to broach* voice
the *things it's wiser not to voice* voice.

Carole Satyamurti

Striking Distance

Was there one moment when the woman
who's always lived next door turned stranger
to you? In a time of fearful weather
did the way she laughed, or shook out her mats
make you suddenly feel as though
she'd been nursing a dark side to her difference
and bring that word, in a bitter rush
to the back of the throat—*Croat / Muslim /
Serb*—the name, barbed, ripping
its neat solution through common ground?

Or has she acquired an alien patina
day by uneasy day, unnoticed
as fall-out from a remote explosion?
So you don't know quite when you came to think
the way she sits, or ties her scarf,
is just like a Muslim / Serb / Croat;
and she uses their word for water-melon
as usual, but now it's an irritant
you mimic to ugliness in your head,
surprising yourself in a savage pleasure.

Do you sometimes think, she could be you,
the woman who's trying to be invisible?
Do you have to betray those old complicities
—money worries, sick children, men?
Would an open door be too much pain
if the larger bravery is beyond you
(you can't afford the kind of recklessness
that would take, any more than she could);
while your husband is saying you don't understand
those people / Serbs / Muslims / Croats?

One morning, will you ignore her greeting
and think you see a strange twist to her smile
—for how could she not, then, be strange to herself
(this woman who lives nine inches away)
in the inner place where she'd felt she belonged,
which, now, she'll return to obsessively
as a tongue tries to limit a secret sore?
And as they drive her away, will her face
be unfamiliar, her voice, bearable:
a woman crying, from a long way off?

Jo Shapcott

Vegetable Love

I'd like to say the fridge
was clean, but look at the rusty
streaks down the back wall
and the dusty brown pools
underneath the salad crisper.

And this is where I've lived
the past two weeks, since I was pulled
from the vegetable garden.
I'm wild for him: I want to stay crunchy
enough to madden his hard palate and his tongue,
every sensitive part inside his mouth.
But almost hour by hour now, it seems,
I can feel my outer leaves losing resistance,
as oxygen leaks in, water leaks out
and the same tendency creeps further
and further towards my heart.

Down here there's not much action,
just me and another, even limper, lettuce
and half an onion. The door opens so many,
so many times a day, but he never opens
the salad drawer where I'm curled in a corner.

There's an awful lot of meat. Strange cuts:
whole limbs with their grubby hair,
wings and thighs of large birds,
claws and beaks. New juice
gathers pungency as it rolls down
through the smelly strata of the refrigerator,
and drips on to our fading heads.

The thermostat is kept as low as it will go,
and when the weather changes
for the worse, what's nearest
to the bottom of the fridge starts to freeze.
Three times we've had cold snaps,
and I've felt the terrifying pain
as ice crystals formed at my fringes.

Insulation isn't everything in here:
you've got to relax into the cold,
let it in at every pore. It's proper
for food preservation. But I heat up
again at the thought of him,
at the thought of mixing into one juice
with his saliva, of passing down his throat
and being ingested with the rest
into his body cells where I'll learn
by osmosis another lovely version
of curl, then shrivel, then open again to desire.

Owen Sheers

Old Horse, New Tricks

The vet was careful
to place the barrel of his gun
right on the swirl of hair
in the centre of her forehead.

In the silence after the explosion
she was still for a second,
as if she would stand in death
as she had stood in sleep.

We watched, an audience expecting tricks,
and eventually she obliged,
succumbing to the slow fold of her fall
with a buckling of the crooked back legs

and a comedy sideways lean that went too far.
There was little symmetry in her collapse,
just the natural pattern of pain.
Even her tongue was out of order,

escaping from the side of her jaw,
and dipping to taste the earth below,
like a child, stealing a taste of the cake
before it is served.

Penelope Shuttle

Outgrown

It is both sad and a relief to fold so carefully
her outgrown clothes and line up the little worn shoes
of childhood, so prudent, scuffed and particular.
It is both happy and horrible to send them galloping
back tappity-tap along the misty chill path into the past.

It is both a freedom and a prison, to be outgrown
by her as she towers over me as thin as a sequin
in her doc martens and her pretty skirt,
because just as I work out how to be a mother
she stops being a child.

George Szirtes

Actually, yes

Somewhere between the highly spectacular *No*
and the modest *yes* of the creatures, word
arises and claims its space. *No* can afford
fireworks and a grand entrance, but *yes* must go
barefoot across floorboards. *No* can extend
its franchise over the glossolalia
of the imagination: *yes* discovers failure
in a preposition impossible to offend.
No demands success and receives reviews
of the utmost luminosity while *yes*
is damned with faint praise. *No* profits by excess:
yes has little to say and even less to lose.
The full Shakespearean ending is *No* with its raised brow.
Yes disappears off stage and will not take a bow.

Look, here's a very small *yes*. Now watch it run
its almost invisible race through nature. How
does it know where to go? Where is it now?
Right there! Just there! Like a picture of no one
in particular it looks surprised to be seeing
itself approach a selfhood hardly likely. See
it hesitate as it approaches the sheer possibility
of emergence on the very edge of being.
Always off-centre, its marginal affirmation
of life's distant provinces will be rewarded
with the briefest of smiles when smiles can be afforded
while monstrous *No* boldly addresses the nation.
But now and then, the honest citizen will confess,
when asked, to a weakness of sorts, whispering *Yes*.

Well, *yes*. Actually, *yes*.

Kate Tempest

Thirteen

The boys have football and skate ramps.
They can ride BMX
and play basketball in the courts by the flats until midnight.
The girls have shame.

One day,
when we are grown and we have minds of our own,
we will be kind women, with nice smiles and families and jobs.
And we will sit,
with the weight of our lives and our pain
pushing our bodies down into the bus seats,
and we will see thirteen-year-old girls for what will seem like the first
    time since we've been them,
and they will be sitting in front of us, laughing
into their hands at our shoes or our jackets,
    and rolling their eyes at each other.

While out of the window, in the sunshine,
the boys will be cheering each other on,
and daring each other to jump higher and higher.

RS Thomas

Geriatric

What god is proud
    of this garden
of dead flowers, this underwater
    grotto of humanity,
where limbs wave in invisible
    currents, faces drooping
on dry stalks, voices clawing
    in a last desperate effort
to retain hold? Despite withered
    petals, I recognise
the species: Charcot, Ménière,
    Alzheimer. There are no gardeners
here, caretakers only
    of reason overgrown
by confusion. This body once,
    when it was in bud,
opened to love's kisses. These eyes,
    cloudy with rheum,
were clear pebbles that love's rivulet
    hurried over. Is this
the best Rabbi Ben Ezra
    promised? I come away
comforting myself, as I can,
    that there is another
garden, all dew and fragrance,
    and that these are the brambles
about it we are caught in,
    a sacrifice prepared
by a torn god to a love fiercer
    than we can understand.

Derek Walcott

White Egrets

I

Cautious of time's light and how often it will allow
the morning shadows to lengthen across the lawn
the stalking egrets to wriggle their beaks and swallow
when you, not they, or you and they, are gone;
for clattering parrots to launch their fleet at sunrise
for April to ignite the African violet
in the drumming world that dampens your tired eyes
behind two clouding lenses, sunrise, sunset,
the quiet ravages of diabetes.
Accept it all with level sentences
with sculpted settlement that sets each stanza,
learn how the bright lawn puts up no defences
against the egret's stabbing questions and the night's answer.

Lucy Anne Watt

The Tree Position

My son went to war in a country the colour of sand. And came back
in a light beech box hefted on the shoulders of six strong men.

And this and my son turned me into a tree.
All the leaves of my happiness fell from me.

I hooked my fingers into the sky and my roots embraced
the last of my son. Earth to earth as they say.

But ash is the taste in my mouth. Ash, the colour of my sky and skin;
of the remains of my love. In parturition I did not scream.

I bit down hard on a towel, a rag, so as better to hear
my boy's first shout. As I embody his last that I never heard.

And I watched the Prime Minister pass. The young PM
aka Warlord, aka Sancho Panza to another's Quixote,

aka Pinball Player with the lives of young men. And I saw in him
    an actor.
An actor can act big while being a fool.

And even with my fingers in the sky, and my roots in cinders,
and rain always in my eyes, strung between

the hell of my love and the heaven of release,
suspended in the perpetual winter

of barrenness reprised,
the PM looked right through me. And I decided

only lawyers think that wars are arguments to be won. But wars are
   always lost.
In the heart. In the home. In the wheelchair. In the widow's tiny
   portion.

In the fatherless child. In mothers
like me. In the compound nature of the cost.

Soldiers obey orders. But where were mine?
When did I contract to be as I now am?

So I cursed the PM. I will not say how. I was one
grieving tree. But the war goes on. I am a forest now.

Hugo Williams

Joy

Not so much a sting
as a faint burn

not so much a pain
as the memory of pain

the memory of tears
flowing freely down cheeks

in a sort of joy
that there was nothing

worse in all the world
than stinging nettle stings

and nothing better
than cool dock leaves.

Benjamin Zephaniah

Man to Man

Macho man
Can't cook
Macho man
Can't sew
Macho man
Eats plenty Red Meat,
At home him is King,
From front garden to back garden
From de lift to de balcony
Him a supreme Master,
Controller.

Food mus ready
On time,
Cloth mus ready
On time,
Woman mus ready
On time,
How Macho can yu go?

Cum
Talk to me bout sexuality,
Cum meditate,
Cum Save de Whale,
Dose bulging muscles need Tai Chi
Yo drunken eyes need herb tea,
Cum, Relax.

Macho man
Can't cook, sew or wash him pants,
But Macho Man is in full control.

Biographies

Moniza Alvi (b. 1954 Lahore, Pakistan) grew up in Hertfordshire, first visiting her birthplace as an adult in the mid-90s. Over eight poetry collections, she has explored all manner of contrasts and divisions, not just those between the east and west of her dual inheritance, but between the physical and the spiritual, the familiar and the surreal. A secondary school teacher in London for many years, she now lives in Norfolk.

Simon Armitage (b. 1963 Yorkshire) yearned to be a rock star but, after a spell as a Manchester probation officer, settled instead for being a poet. He has written for radio, television, film and stage: his work delights audiences of all ages. He became Oxford University's professor of poetry in 2015. The poem included here was inspired by one of his student's stories about finding a copy of Ezra Pound's letters in Poundland.

Mona Arshi (b. 1970 London) worked for years as a human rights lawyer: her cases included that of the 'right-to-die' campaigner Diane Pretty. Born into a family of Punjabi Sikhs in Hounslow, she uses humour, pathos and a wide range of poetic forms. Her 2015 book, *Small Hands*, won the Forward Prize for Best First Collection.

Ros Barber (b. 1964 Washington DC, USA) grew up in Essex and combines poetry with scholarship. Her academic research into the question of Shakespearean authorship fed into her prize-winning verse novel *The Marlowe Papers*. She has published three collections: one, *Material*, contains poems written after the death of her mother in a freak accident while on holiday in Thailand.

George Barker (b. 1913 Essex; d. 1991) was declared a genius at the age of 22 by TS Eliot and conformed closely to the image of poets as 'mad, bad and dangerous to know'. His 1965 masterpiece *The True Confession of George Barker*, broadcast on BBC Radio, was denounced as 'pornography' in the House of Lords. Despite addiction to drink and drugs and a habit of violence, he fathered 15 children with four women – including the writer Elizabeth Smart – and died at the age of 78 in Norfolk.

Fiona Benson (b. 1978 Wiltshire) has said about her work: 'I often feel I am breaching terrible taboos.' Her prize-winning first collection *Bright Travellers* – praised for its 'sharp intelligence pushing itself into some uncomfortable and upsetting emotional places' – includes sequences on miscarriage, childbirth and motherhood. She declares: 'I am interested in getting the female experience in all its diversity down on the page.'

Judi Benson (b. 1947 California, USA) is an artist and anthologist. After the death of her husband, the poet Ken Smith, she spent two years as writer-in-residence at Dumfries and Galloway Royal Infirmary, working in oncology and palliative care. *Hole in the Wall* is an examination of the effects of death on those left behind. She now lives in London.

Emily Berry (b. 1981 London) won acclaim – and a Forward Prize – for her debut collection, *Dear Boy*, in which struggles for power and love are dramatized in fragmented monologues. 'Letter to Husband' is based on the story of a woman who wrote repeatedly to her husband from a mental hospital: 'They were never sent, and he never came, so she seemed to be in this kind of frozen state of yearning.' She cites John Berryman as an important influence.

Liz Berry (b. 1980 West Midlands) worked as an infant school teacher, before studying for a creative writing MA at Royal Holloway. She was awarded an Eric Gregory Award in 2009, publishing her Forward Prize-winning debut collection, *Black Country*, in 2014. Her work is distinctive for its use of Black Country dialect, as she wanted, she says, 'to reclaim it as something beautiful to be treasured and celebrated'. She lives in Birmingham.

Kate Bingham (b. 1971 London) is the author of three poetry collections, two novels, an illustrated children's alphabet and several screenplays. The *Guardian* wrote: 'Her poems celebrate love's beauty and essentialness, but are clear-eyed about its realities: co-dependence, moments of ugliness, the fact its end is inherent in the moment of its inception.'

Eavan Boland (b. 1944 Dublin) was educated in London, New York and Dublin. She published her first book of poems while an undergraduate.

She has taught in Ireland and the USA, and is currently a professor at Stanford University. 'Inheritance' is from *Domestic Violence*, a collection that considers the everyday and mythical aspects of contemporary women's lives.

Pat Boran (b. 1963 Portlaoise) has written over a dozen books of poetry and prose. He directed the Dublin Writers Festival, and is a teacher of creative writing and the author of *The Portable Creative Writing Workshop*. He is a regular contributor to several radio programmes and, since 2005, has worked for the poetry publisher Dedalus. 'Waving' is from his second collection, *Familiar Things*.

Kamau Brathwaite (b. 1930 Bridgetown, Barbados) graduated from Pembroke College, Cambridge, in 1953. He taught in Ghana, the West Indies and the USA, latterly as a professor of comparative literature at New York University. He has served on the board of UNESCO's History of Mankind project since 1979. His poetry, featuring jazz rhythms and dialect, traces the development of the black population in the Caribbean.

Colette Bryce (b. 1970 Derry) left Northern Ireland for England aged 18. She won the National Poetry Competition in 2003 with 'The Full Indian Rope Trick', has held writing fellowships in Dundee and north-east England, and was poetry editor of *Poetry London* from 2009 to 2013. Her work has been described as 'a set of necessary, hard-won, and thoroughly secular myths for the present day'.

John Burnside (b. 1955 Dunfermline) emerged from a troubled upbringing in Fife, via bad LSD trips, psychiatric wards and insanity, to become first a software engineer, then a celebrated writer and professor. He brought out his first collection of poetry in his thirties: since then his poems, novels and memoirs have won him a devoted following and many prizes. Poetry, he says, is 'a defence of care over the language, its richness, its subtleties, its possibilities'.

Matthew Caley (b. 1959 Nottingham) worked as a record sleeve designer in Newcastle upon Tyne, before moving to London. His fifth collection, *Rake*, was published by Bloodaxe Books, and his work has appeared in many anthologies including Roddy Lumsden's *Identity Parade*. He co-edited *Pop Fiction: The Song in Cinema* with Steve Lannin, and works at London Metropolitan University.

Vahni Capildeo (b. 1973 Port of Spain, Trinidad) attributes her interest in words' music and meanings to a childhood that required constant navigation between English, Spanish, Hindi, French, Sanskrit and various creoles. After winning a Rhodes Scholarship to Oxford University, she took a DPhil in Old Norse and worked on the Oxford English Dictionary. She has published six collections. 'Language,' she says, 'is my home.'

Anne Carson (b. 1950 Toronto, Canada) learned Greek during her lunch hour at high school, which led to a career teaching classics at several major North American universities. As well as translating writers such as Sappho and Euripides, Carson – whose work has been described as 'unclassifiable' – has published poems, libretti, verse novels and works of criticism. In 2001 she was the first woman to win the TS Eliot Prize.

Ciaran Carson (b. 1948 Belfast) was reared bilingually, speaking Irish at home, English outside. For many years he was traditional arts officer for the Arts Council of Northern Ireland, and latterly professor of English at Queen's University Belfast. He has published many poetry collections, a novel and a book on Irish music, and his acclaimed translations include Dante's *Divine Comedy*. 'Alibi' is a set of translations from the Romanian poet Stefan Doinas into Irish ballad metre.

Kate Clanchy (b. 1965 Glasgow) was the first Oxford City Poet (2011–13). She taught in London's East End, before moving to Oxford, where she works as a broadcaster and teacher and writes award-winning short stories, novels, poetry and non-fiction. As poet-in-residence at Oxford Spires Academy, she has mentored a generation of young and diverse writers. A documentary about their poetry was shortlisted for the 2016 Ted Hughes Award.

Gillian Clarke (b. 1937 Cardiff) edited *The Anglo-Welsh Review* from 1975 to 1984. She founded and is president of Tŷ Newydd, the writers' centre in North Wales, and was the National Poet of Wales from

2008 to 2016. She currently runs an organic small-holding in Ceredigion. 'Anorexic' is from *The King of Britain's Daughter*, the text of an oratorio based on the story of Branwen, the daughter of Llŷr, from the *Mabinogion*.

Wendy Cope (b. 1945 Kent) exchanged teaching in London primary schools for a writing career in 1986 when her first collection, *Making Cocoa for Kingsley Amis*, became a bestseller. Her witty lyrics and pitch-perfect parodies have earned her a devoted following. Awarded an OBE in 2010, she lives in Winchester.

Robert Crawford (b. 1959 Lanarkshire) is one of the 1994 'New Generation' poets and a co-founder of the magazine *Verse*. His recurrent themes as a poet are technology and Scotland; he has described his homeland as a 'semiconductor country' of 'intimate expanses'. He is a prolific critic and anthologist, and biographer of Burns and TS Eliot.

Allan Crosbie (b. 1968 Bermuda) grew up in Scotland. After graduating from St Andrew's University, he completed a masters in peace studies in the USA during the Gulf War, and worked with repatriated refugees in El Salvador. *Outswimming the Eruption* was shortlisted for the Jerwood Aldeburgh First Collection Prize. He works as a secondary school teacher in Edinburgh.

Kwame Dawes (b. 1962 Ghana) grew up in Jamaica, studied in Canada, lived and worked in South Carolina, and now teaches English at the University of Nebraska. An actor, broadcaster, playwright, novelist and singer, his works include a memoir of his years in Jamaica, Biblical epics, reggae poems and a book about Bob Marley. 'New Neighbours' is from his first book, *Progeny of Air*, winner of a 1994 Forward Prize.

Imtiaz Dharker (b. 1954 Lahore, Pakistan) grew up in Glasgow as, in her words, a 'Scottish Muslim Calvinist'. An artist and film-maker, she has published six poetry collections and won the Queen's Gold Medal for Poetry in 2014. Through her readings with Poetry Live, founded by her late husband, Simon Powell, she reaches 25,000 school children a year.

Michael Donaghy (b. 1954 New York, USA; d. 2004) studied at Fordham and Chicago Universities before moving to London in 1985, where his charisma and acute critical eye influenced a generation of young poets. A musician, his works feature a wide range of musical references from Irish ballads to Purcell and Mozart. At readings he recited his complex, allusive poems entirely from memory. He died suddenly at the age of 50.

Tishani Doshi (b. 1975 Madras, India) is a writer and dancer of Welsh-Gujarati origin, who has published essays, newspaper columns, poems, short stories and a novel. After studying in the USA, she worked in fashion in London. In 2001, she returned to India where she became a dancer with the choreographer Chandralekha. She lives in Tamil Nadu.

Jane Draycott (b. 1954 London) has a particular interest in sound art and collaborative work. *Tideway* features poems, with paintings by Peter Hay, about London's working watermen, written during a residency at Henley's River & Rowing Museum. *Pearl* is her prize-winning translation of the visionary medieval poem. A poet of concision and careful craft, she lectures at Oxford and Lancaster Universities.

Carol Ann Duffy (b. 1955 Glasgow) is one of Britain's most admired and popular poets, whose poems are at once accessible and brilliantly idiosyncratic and subtle. *The World's Wife* explores and subverts female archetypes, while *Rapture* charts the joys and agonies of a love affair. She has written extensively for the theatre. In 2009 she was appointed poet laureate. She lives in Manchester.

Ian Duhig (b. 1954 London) was born to Irish Gaelic-speaking parents. He studied in Leeds, and worked for many years with homeless people. He won the National Poetry Competition – for the second time – with 'The Lammas Hireling', the title poem of a prize-winning collection set in Northumbria, which contains a blend of 'border ballads, dark psychology and biting wit'. He lives in Leeds.

Helen Dunmore (b. 1952 Yorkshire) studied English at York University and then taught for two years in Finland. Her debut collection, *The Apple*

Fall, was one of the first titles published by Bloodaxe Books. Her writing – fiction and poetry – is notable for its rich vein of imagery depicting the natural world, food and bodily pleasures.

UA Fanthorpe (b. 1929 London; d. 2009) taught English at Cheltenham Ladies' College, but left in her forties to work in a hospital, and to write. Her first collection, *Side Effects*, appeared when she was almost 50. A popular and much-loved poet, her work is full of wit and sly debunking of national myth.

Paul Farley (b. 1965 Liverpool) studied at Chelsea School of Art. He was poet-in-residence at Dove Cottage, and now lectures in creative writing at the University of Lancaster. He contributes regularly to BBC Radio. His books include *Edgelands*, a prize-winning appreciation of marginal landscapes, with poet Michael Symmons Roberts, and a study of Terence Davies' film *Distant Voices, Still Lives*.

Vicki Feaver (b. 1943 Nottingham) grew up 'in a house of quarrelling women'. She studied music at Durham University, and later taught creative writing at the University of Chichester. Her distinctive and highly regarded work, which often deals with the repression of female creativity, has been described as 'domestic gothic…by turns poignant or sinister'. She lives in South Lanarkshire.

Duncan Forbes (b. 1947 Oxford) read English at university and later taught in various secondary schools. He has been described as 'a poet of many moods: elegiac, hedonistic, flippant, caustic, comically fanciful and wistfully puzzled'. His first poetry collection, *August Autumn*, was published in 1984 by Secker and Warburg. Enitharmon has published a further four collections.

Linda France (b. 1958 Newcastle upon Tyne) edited the anthology *Sixty Women Poets*. Her own poetry collections include *The Toast of the Kit-Cat Club*, a verse biography of the eighteenth-century traveller Lady Mary Wortley Montagu. 'Bernard and Cerinthe', described in one newspaper as 'a sexy poem about a plant', won the 2013 National Poetry Competition. She lives in Northumberland.

Matthew Francis (b. 1955 Hampshire) worked in IT for a decade, before studying for a PhD in English at Southampton University. He lives in West Wales and lectures at Aberystwyth University. His poems can be at once fantastical and historically grounded, as in *Mandeville*, based on the unlikely adventures recounted in a fourteenth-century travel journal.

Pamela Gillilan (b. 1918 London; d. 2001) wrote poems and fiction as a young woman, and served as a WAAF meteorologist with Bomber Command during World War Two. She met her future husband, David, on a train in Switzerland, and the couple ran a restoration business in Cornwall. His death in 1974 prompted her return to poetry. Her last book, *The Rashomon Syndrome*, features poems on family relationships and the delusions of memory.

Alan Gillis (b. 1973 Belfast) studied in Dublin and Belfast, and lectures at Edinburgh University. As a teenager he planned to write songs and be in a band, but turned to poetry instead. He has published four collections, several critical works on Irish poetry, and edits *Edinburgh Review*. His poems, it has been said, are 'littered with the traces of life at its sweetest'.

John Goodby (b. 1958 Birmingham) is a critic, poet, translator and arts organiser. He has written extensively on Dylan Thomas, and edited the new annotated edition of Thomas's *Collected Poems*. 'The Uncles' won the 2006 Cardiff International Poetry Competition. He is a member of Boiled String, a multi-media group who present innovative poetic works. He lives in Swansea.

Lavinia Greenlaw (b. 1962 London) grew up in a family of scientists. She has held residencies at the Royal Festival Hall, the Royal Society of Medicine and the Science Museum; the latter inspired several poems in her second collection, *A World Where News Travelled Slowly*. Her radio work includes programmes about light, involving trips to the Arctic in midsummer and midwinter, and to the darkest place in England.

Thom Gunn (b. 1929 Kent; d. 2004) studied English at Cambridge under FR Leavis. He moved to California with his partner Mike Kitay shortly after publishing his first, much-praised collection in 1954. *The Man with Night Sweats* deals with the effects of the AIDS epidemic on the gay community, and includes major poems about mutability and mortality, endurance and celebration.

Jen Hadfield (b. 1978 Cheshire) studied in Edinburgh and Glasgow, and travelled to the Western Isles and Canada before settling in Shetland. She was the youngest writer to win the TS Eliot Prize, which she won for her second collection *Nigh-No-Place*. Rooted in Shetland, her work is characterised by originality, astonishment and adoration. She also makes paintings and sculptures, using found and salvaged materials.

Tony Harrison (b. 1937 Leeds) studied classics and linguistics, and in the 1960s worked in Nigeria and Czechoslovakia. His controversial poem 'V.', broadcast on Channel 4 in 1987, was denounced for obscenity in the House of Commons. He has written extensively for the theatre, reworking classic French and Greek dramas to great acclaim: his triumphs include a powerful version of *The Oresteia* for the National Theatre. *A Cold Coming* features poems about the Gulf War.

David Harsent (b. 1942 Devon) has published 11 poetry collections: the most recent, *Fire Songs*, won the TS Eliot Prize. He has written opera libretti for composer Harrison Birtwistle, and detective novels under the pseudonyms Jack Curtis and David Lawrence. *Sprinting to the Graveyard* includes his versions of poems by Goran Simi, written during the siege of Sarajevo.

Seamus Heaney (b. 1939 County Derry; d. 2013) is widely recognized as one of the major poets of the twentieth century. A native of Northern Ireland, he was raised in County Derry and later lived for many years in Dublin. He won the Nobel Prize in Literature in 1995 'for works of lyrical beauty and ethical depth, which exalt everyday miracles and the living past'. Heaney was Oxford professor of poetry (1989-94).

Stuart Henson (b. 1954 Huntingdonshire) taught at Kimbolton School in Cambridgeshire, where he and fellow poet John Greening ran a series of poetry readings in the saloon of Kimbolton Castle. A playwright as well as a poet, his work has been described as 'strongly muscled [and] nervily responsive to his environment'. He has published five collections of poems, most recently *The Odin Stone*.

WN Herbert (b. 1961 Dundee) studied English at Oxford, completing his PhD on the work of Hugh MacDiarmid. Like MacDiarmid, Herbert writes in both Scots and English. He describes himself as a 'polystylist' who is 'obsessed by how different modes of writing interact – not just Scots or English, but also formal or free verse, poetry on the page or in performance, long poems, forty-line lyrics'.

Geoffrey Hill (b. 1932 Worcestershire; d. 2016) wrote poetry and criticism distinguished for its seriousness, its high moral tone, extreme allusiveness and dedication to history, theology and philosophy. He said: 'In my view, difficult poetry is the most democratic, because you are doing your audience the honour of supposing that they are intelligent human beings.' He was Oxford professor of poetry (2010-15) and was knighted in 2012.

Selima Hill (b. 1945 London) grew up in rural England and Wales, and read moral sciences at Cambridge. The often difficult subject matter of her poems – sexual abuse, mental illness, family conflicts – is offset by humour, whimsy and a wide variety of wonderfully odd imagery. She has worked with the Royal Ballet and Welsh National Opera, and taught creative writing in hospitals and prisons. She lives in Dorset.

Ellen Hinsey (b. 1960 Boston, USA) has lived in Europe since 1987, based mainly in Paris. Her first collection, *Cities of Memory*, considers key twentieth-century events, including the building, and collapse, of the Berlin Wall. *Update on the Descent* draws on her experiences attending the International Criminal Tribunal for the Former Yugoslavia in The Hague, and considers tyranny, violence and civil division, as well as the possibility of reconciliation.

Sarah Howe (b. 1983 Hong Kong) moved to the UK as a child, with her English father and Chinese mother. She studied English at Cambridge University and won a scholarship to Harvard. Her inventive, erudite and formally adventurous book *Loop of Jade* was the first debut collection to win the TS Eliot Prize, in 2016.

Ted Hughes (b. 1930 Yorkshire; d. 1998) met the American poet Sylvia Plath at Cambridge University; they married in 1956. Her suicide in 1963 overshadowed the rest of his life. He wrote many successful books after her death – including the fragmentary epic *Crow*, the children's book *The Iron Man* and *Tales from Ovid* – but none created such public interest as *Birthday Letters*, containing poems written to Plath over the previous 35 years.

Clive James (b. 1939 Sydney, Australia) moved to England in 1962. For ten years he was the television critic for the *Observer*, and became a regular on television himself. His autobiography, *Unreliable Memoirs*, was hugely popular, and he has also written novels, essay collections, several books of poetry, a translation of Dante's *Divine Comedy* and song lyrics (with Pete Atkin). He was diagnosed with leukemia in 2010.

Kathleen Jamie (b. 1962 Renfrewshire) published her first collection, *Black Spiders*, at the age of 20. Throughout her career she has used Scots, sometimes sparingly, sometimes more intensively, as in 'Speirin'. Ecological concerns have become prominent in her recent poems and essays. She lives in Fife, and teaches at the University of Stirling.

Alan Jenkins (b. 1955 Kingston upon Thames) grew up in London, and has worked for the *Times Literary Supplement* since 1981. He writes poems of intense feelings – sexual jealousy, romantic regret, elegiac contemplation, and grief. Elegies for his father in his early collections were followed in *A Shorter Life* by poems about his widowed, dying mother. *Drunken Boats*, a translation of Rimbaud, appeared in 2007.

Linton Kwesi Johnson (b. 1952 Chapelton, Jamaica) moved to London in 1963. He presents his unashamedly political work – often written in Jamaican patois – in books, on stage, and as recordings. In the 1980s, he founded his own record label, LKJ records. When *Mi Revalueshanary Fren* was published by Penguin Classics in 2002 he was the second living poet to appear in the series.

Jackie Kay (b. 1961 Edinburgh) was born to a Scottish mother and a Nigerian father, and raised in Glasgow by her adoptive parents. Her first book, *The Adoption Papers*, dramatized her story in the voices of the birth mother, adoptive mother, and daughter. Her work, which includes poems, short stories, a novel and work for children, has been praised for its 'clear, plain style, and its fearless spoken poignancy'. In 2016 she was appointed the Scottish Makar.

Mimi Khalvati (b. 1944 Tehran, Iran) grew up on the Isle of Wight, and was educated in Switzerland and London. She worked in theatre in the UK and Iran, founded the Poetry School in London in 1997, and, in 2000, was poet-in-residence with the Royal Mail. Her work relishes the musicality of language. As she has said: 'I am trying to move closer to song.'

John Kinsella (b. 1963 Perth, Australia) is a poet, novelist, critic, publisher and journal editor. His poetry is both experimental and pastoral, featuring the landscape of Western Australia. He describes himself as a 'vegan anarchist pacifist...a supporter of worldwide indigenous rights, and an absolute supporter of land rights'.

August Kleinzahler (b. 1949 New Jersey, USA) studied at the University of Victoria in Canada under Basil Bunting. He credits his many jobs – including locksmith, cab driver, lumberjack and building manager – with keeping him 'out of the academy, which saved me'. Latterly, he has taught creative writing in California and Iowa. His 'inventive recklessness with words' is balanced by a control of form which Allen Ginsberg called 'precise, concrete, intelligent and rare'. He lives in San Francisco.

RF Langley (b. 1938 Warwickshire; d. 2011) was an English teacher for nearly 40 years, at schools in Wolverhampton and Sutton Coldfield. His *Collected Poems*, published in 2000, contains only 17 poems, but when he retired to rural Suffolk, where many of his poems are set, he became more productive. His work – the poems and *Journals* – is founded on careful, close observation of things that typically pass unnoticed.

James Lasdun (b. 1958 London) has lived in the Catskill Mountains of New York State since 1985. He has taught creative writing at Columbia, Princeton and New York Universities, and published poetry, fiction, guidebooks and screenplays. *Give Me Everything You Have: On Being Stalked* is a memoir describing a harrowing ordeal at the hands of a former student. 'Stones' shows the poet 'in two minds about the kind of ingeniously crafted verse he often writes'.

Gwyneth Lewis (b. 1959 Cardiff) writes in both Welsh and English. She studied English at Cambridge and Harvard, later working as a journalist in New York, and on TV documentaries for BBC Wales. She was Wales's first National Poet (2005-2006): her words in letters six feet high can be seen on the Wales Millennium Centre in Cardiff.

Michael Longley (b. 1939 Belfast) read classics at Trinity College, Dublin, and worked for 20 years for the Arts Council of Northern Ireland, becoming a freelance writer in 1991. While his early poems are marked by an unflinching engagement with the Northern Irish Troubles, his later poems, often minimalist, show him to be a quiet, punctilious observer of love and landscape. He lives in Belfast.

Hannah Lowe (b. 1976 Essex) was born to an English mother and Jamaican-Chinese father, nicknamed 'Chick', who was a professional gambler. She began to write when he died, and the poems in *Chick* are attempts to piece together his experiences in London, and beyond. She has also written a memoir of her father, *Long Time No See*, a second poetry collection, *Chan*, and two pamphlets, *Rx* and *Ormonde*.

Roddy Lumsden (b. 1966 St Andrews) studied in Edinburgh, where he lived for many years before moving to London. A poet, editor and poetry teacher, whose work is notable for its melancholy and self-examination, fractured narratives and formal inventiveness, he also writes quizzes and word puzzles. His book on poetry and pop music, *The Message*, grew out of a Poetry Society residency with the music industry.

Derek Mahon (b. 1941 Belfast) studied French in Dublin and Paris. He lived and worked in North America before moving to London, where he wrote reviews, and screenplays for the BBC. A translator of French poetry and plays (including *Cyrano de Bergerac*), his poetry has been praised for its 'lucid, sculpted lines [which] incorporate both classical allusion and contemporary life'.

Glyn Maxwell (b. 1962 Welwyn Garden City) read English at Oxford, before studying poetry and drama at Boston University with Derek Walcott. He moved to the USA in 1996 to teach at Amherst College, Massachusetts. The funny, wry and multi-faceted poems in *Pluto* are his most directly personal work to date.

Roger McGough (b. 1937 Liverpool) studied at Hull University before lecturing at the Liverpool College of Art. A member of the music and poetry group The Scaffold for ten years, he was one of the Liverpool Poets (with Adrian Henri and Brian Patten) featured in the million-selling Penguin anthology *The Mersey Sound*. His work delights both children and adults: it is often extremely funny. He is a regular presenter of BBC Radio 4's Poetry Please.

Jamie McKendrick (b. 1955 Liverpool) studied at Nottingham University and taught in Italy at the University of Salerno. He lives in Oxford, where he teaches as well as reviewing poetry and the visual arts for newspapers and magazines. His poems have been described as 'caught between humour and alarm'. He translates from Italian, and edited *The Faber Book of 20th-Century Italian Poems*.

Kei Miller (b. 1978 Kingston, Jamaica) studied at the University of the West Indies, and at Manchester Metropolitan University where he financed the first days of his MA studies with poetry slam prize money. In his Forward Prize winning collection, *The Cartographer Tries to Map a Way to Zion*, he turns his wit and lively, satirical intelligence on conflicting methods of knowing, and thus owning, a place. A novelist, short-story writer and academic, he has a doctorate from Glasgow University and teaches at Royal Holloway.

Sinéad Morrissey (b. 1972 County Armagh) has lived and worked in Japan and New Zealand. In 2003 she travelled through China as part of the British Council's Writers' Train Project. Now a professor at Queen's University, Belfast, her poetry balances spiritual and literary allusions, and is as much international as local, with Belfast as its hub; she was appointed the city's first poet laureate in 2014.

Paul Muldoon (b. 1951 County Armagh) was taught at Queen's University, Belfast, by Seamus Heaney, and published his first book, *New Weather*, aged only 21. He worked for the BBC in Northern Ireland until moving to the USA, where, since 1987, he has been a professor at Princeton University. His poetry is marked by great inventiveness with rhyme and a love of dazzling wordplay.

Les Murray (b. 1938 Nabiac, Australia) grew up on a dairy farm at Bunyah, NSW. He studied modern languages at Sydney University, and lived in the city for many years until returning to Bunyah in 1985. A convert to Roman Catholicism, his work often contrasts provocatively the 'imported idiocies' of the cities with the 'quality of sprawl', which he identifies as the essential Australian characteristic.

Daljit Nagra (b. 1966 London) grew up in London and Sheffield, the son of Punjabi Sikhs who came from India in the late 1950s. Inspired by the work of William Blake, he returned to London in 1988 to study at Royal Holloway, though he only started writing seriously on turning 30. Many of his poems are written in 'Punglish', a 'neologism-infused blend of English and Punjabi'.

Sean O'Brien (b. 1952 London) grew up in Hull, taught at Sheffield Hallam University and is now a professor at Newcastle University. A poet, playwright, essayist, novelist and anthologist, he has created in his work a personal – often bleak, elegiac and angry – vision of northern England. He has adapted novels for BBC Radio, including Yevgeny Zamyatin's *We* and Graham Greene's *Ministry of Fear*.

Alice Oswald (b. 1966 Reading) read classics at Oxford University. Her writing is informed by classical literature, an acute awareness of nature and by her skill as a gardener, and has been described as 'visionary' and 'incantatory'. The book-length *Dart* is a many-voiced poem composed from years of conversations with people along the River Dart, while *Memorial* is a contemporary evocation of the dead from *The Iliad*. She lives in Devon.

Don Paterson (b. 1963 Dundee) lived and worked as a musician in London for many years before returning to Scotland in 1993. His early collections were praised for blending 'technical dexterity, hardline scepticism and outlandish humour'. His work encompasses versions of Machado and Rilke, a study of Shakespeare's sonnets and two books of epigrams. He is the poetry editor for Picador, teaches at St Andrews University, and lives in Dundee.

Clare Pollard (b. 1978 Bolton) wrote her first book, *The Heavy-Petting Zoo*, while still at school; these poems described 'what it's like to be young, slim and pissed at the door of the 21st century'. She has written stage and radio plays, and been involved in various translation projects, including Ovid's *Heroines*, which toured as a one-woman theatre show. She works as an editor, journalist and teacher, and lives in London.

Peter Porter (b. 1929 Brisbane, Australia; d. 2010) came to England in 1951, and lived for most of the rest of his life in London. During the 1960s he worked in an advertising agency, and wrote for the *Observer*. A prolific poet, he published two volumes of *Collected Poems*. Further collections followed in the 2000s, when he also recorded a series of radio dialogues with Clive James, reflecting on their lives in poetry.

Sheenagh Pugh (b. 1950 Birmingham) lived in Cardiff for many years, teaching creative writing at the University of Glamorgan. She is a poet, novelist and translator (from German, French and Ancient Greek). *Stonelight* includes the sequence 'The Arctic Chart' about Sir John Franklin's failed expedition seeking the Northwest Passage. 'Envying Owen Beattie' imagines the archaeologist who later excavated the frozen corpses of members of the expedition. She lives in Shetland.

Claudia Rankine (b. 1963 Kingston, Jamaica) studied and teaches in the USA, currently at Yale University. Her work explores 'the unsettled territory between poetry and prose, between the word and the visual image'. Her Forward Prize winning collection *Citizen: An American Lyric* combines poetry, prose, graphic art and photography on the theme of racism.

Denise Riley (b. 1948 Carlisle) has said she uses poetry as 'a way of thinking aloud in a way which is open; not intrusively autobiographical but undefended'. As a feminist philosopher, her academic work engages with the issues of identity, motherhood and employment policies for women in post-war Britain. She has been professor of literature and philosophy at the University of East Anglia and a writer-in-residence at the Tate Gallery, London.

Michael Symmons Roberts (b. 1963 Lancashire) read philosophy and theology at Oxford University, where he converted from atheism to Roman Catholicism. He worked for many years at the BBC, latterly as head of development for BBC Religion & Ethics: his poetry is informed by a fierce moral intelligence. His collaborations with the composer James MacMillan include song cycles, choral works and operas. He is currently professor of poetry at Manchester Metropolitan University.

Robin Robertson (b. 1955 Scone) studied in Aberdeen, before forging a successful career in London as an editor for Jonathan Cape. Over 40 when his first book of poems appeared, he has spoken of the 'frictional' relationship between his job and writing poems. His poetry has been described as 'sensuousness transfused with subtle violence'. He has written versions of poems by Ovid, Baudelaire and Neruda, among others.

Jacob Sam-La Rose (b. 1976 London) has been described as 'a one-man literary industry…passionate about poetry and its power to change people's lives'. He is a performer, editor, co-ordinator and professor of poetry at Guildhall. His poems explore ritual and tradition, hybridity, science fiction, coding and aspects of popular culture, drawing particularly upon comic book narratives, gaming and electronica.

Ann Sansom (b. 1951 Nottinghamshire) tutors regularly for WEA, The Poetry Society and the Arvon Foundation, and is a director of The Poetry Business, which publishes *The North* magazine and

Smith/Doorstop books. 'Voice' appeared in her first collection, *Romance*, and was included in the first issue of Russian *Vogue* in 1999. Her work has been praised as 'an authentic Northern mix of realism and imagination'.

Carole Satyamurti (b. 1939 Kent) has lived in North America, Singapore and Uganda. A poet and sociologist, she taught for many years at the Tavistock Clinic, the Arvon Foundation and The Poetry Society. She co-edited *Acquainted with the Night: Psychoanalysis and the Poetic Imagination* and, in 2015, won the Roehampton Prize for her masterful retelling of the great Sanskrit epic, the Mahabharata. She lives in London.

Jo Shapcott (b. 1953 London) studied at Dublin, Oxford and Harvard, later working in London at Southbank Centre and for the Arts Council. She has worked with many composers, and in the early 2000s, during the BBC Proms season, she presented weekly Poetry Proms on BBC Radio 3. Her poems, witty in their intellectual conceits, give unexpected voice to all kinds of animate and inanimate objects.

Owen Sheers (b. 1974 Suva, Fiji) is a Welsh poet, author and scriptwriter. He wrote and presented *A Poet's Guide to Britain* for BBC4, while for the National Theatre of Wales he wrote *The Passion*, a 72-hour site-specific production in Port Talbot starring and directed by Michael Sheen. In 2012 he was artist-in-residence for the Welsh Rugby Union, and wrote *Calon* about his experiences with the Welsh team.

Penelope Shuttle (b. 1947 Middlesex) has lived in Cornwall since 1970. After writing several novels, she published her first collection of poems in 1980, *The Orchard Upstairs*. Married to the poet Peter Redgrove, she wrote two books with him – one, *The Wise Wound*, about menstruation and creativity – while her collection *Redgrove's Wife* laments and celebrates his life. Her poetry has been praised for displaying resourcefulness, dexterity and impressive imagination.

George Szirtes (b. 1948 Budapest, Hungary) came to England as a refugee in 1956. After studying painting in Leeds and London, he taught art and English in schools for many years, before establishing the creative writing course at Norwich School of Art and Design. His poetry, described as 'rich in the observed and relished phenomena of everyday', often deals with both his homeland and his adopted home; he is also a translator of Hungarian poetry.

Kate Tempest (b. 1985 London) grew up in south-east London. Initially a rapper, she toured the spoken word circuit for a number of years and began writing for theatre in 2012. Her album *Everybody Down* was nominated for the 2014 Mercury Prize. Her published work includes albums, playscripts and collections of poems. *Hold Your Own* looks at contemporary society through the myth of blinded prophet Tiresias.

RS Thomas (b. 1913 Cardiff; d. 2000) grew up in an English-speaking household, and learned Welsh as an adult. He worked as an Anglican priest in several rural, Welsh-speaking parishes, and his earlier work is rooted in the harsh realities of the depopulated hill country. His later work, written after he retired from the church in 1978, often explores interior worlds of private doubt in the search for consolation.

Derek Walcott (b. 1930 Castries, Saint Lucia) has been described as 'the postcolonial poet par excellence'. His work, particularly his 1990 masterpiece *Omeros*, rejoices in what he calls the 'privilege' afforded his generation of Caribbean writers 'of writing about places and people for the first time' while drawing freely on the tradition of canonical English and classical literature. He was awarded the Nobel Prize in Literature in 1992.

Lucy Anne Watt (b. 1951) trained as a teacher and a secretary, and worked for a time renovating houses and gardens in Dorset. Her poems appeared widely in the 1980s in publications including the *London Review of Books*, *Poetry Review* and the *New Statesman*, and in the anthology *New Chatto Poets: Number Two*. She is the author of a novel, *Micawber's Ailment*.

Hugo Williams (b. 1942 Windsor) was born to actors Hugh Williams and Margaret Vyner. Educated at Eton, he worked for the *London*

Magazine, and later wrote theatre, music and TV reviews. His poems have been praised for their openness, pitch-perfect tone and humour. Poetry, for him, is an opportunity to say the unsayable: 'a search for meaning rather than an extension of existing thoughts'.

Benjamin Zephaniah (b. 1958 Birmingham) first performed his own poetry in church aged 10. He left school at 13, unable to read or write, and spent time as a teenager in prison for burglary: these experiences cemented his conviction that poetry has a duty to speak for and to those who do not read books.

Publisher acknowledgements

The poems in this anthology are reprinted from the following books, all by permission of the publishers listed unless stated otherwise. Every effort has been made to trace the copyright holders of the poems published in this book. The editor and publisher apologise if any material has been included without permission or without the appropriate acknowledgement, and would be glad to be told of anyone who has not been consulted. Thanks are due to all the copyright holders cited below for their kind permission:

Moniza Alvi · *Split World: Poems 1990-2005* · Bloodaxe Books · 2005

Simon Armitage · *Paper Aeroplane, Poems Old and New* · Faber & Faber · 2014 · by permission of the publisher and David Godwin Associates Ltd

Mona Arshi · *Small Hands* · Pavilion Poetry · 2015 · by permission of Liverpool University Press

Ros Barber · *Material* · Anvil Press Poetry · 2003 · by permission of Carcanet

George Barker · *Selected Poems* · Faber & Faber · 1995

Judi Benson · *The Thin Places* · The Rockingham Press · 2006 · by permission of the author

Fiona Benson · *Bright Travellers* · Cape Poetry · 2014

Emily Berry · *Dear Boy* · Faber & Faber · 2013

Liz Berry · *Black Country* · Chatto & Windus · 2014

Kate Bingham · *Quicksand Beach* · Seren · 2006

Eavan Boland · *Domestic Violence* · Carcanet · WW Norton · 2007

Pat Boran · *Familiar Things* · Dedalus Press · 1993

Kamau Brathwaite · *Words Need Love Too* · Salt · 2000

Colette Bryce · *The Whole & Rain-domed Universe* · Picador Poetry · 2014

John Burnside · *The Light Trap* · Cape Poetry · 2002

Matthew Caley · *Thirst* · Slow Dancer · 1999 · by permission of the author

Vahni Capildeo · *Measures of Expatriation* · Carcanet · 2016

Ciaran Carson · *Opera et Cetera* · 1996 · by kind permission of the author and The Gallery Press, Loughcrew, Oldcastle, County Meath, Ireland

Anne Carson · *Glass, Irony and God* · New Directions · 1995

Kate Clanchy · *Samarkand* · Picador Poetry· 1999

Gillian Clarke · *The King of Britain's Daughter* · Carcanet · 1993

Wendy Cope · *Serious Concerns* · Faber & Faber · 2002

Robert Crawford · *The Tip of My Tongue* · Cape Poetry · 2003

Allan Crosbie · *Outswimming the Eruption* · Rialto · 2006 · by permission of the author

Kwame Dawes · *Progeny of Air* · Peepal Tree Press · 1994

Imtiaz Dharker · *The terrorist at my table* · Bloodaxe Books · 2006

Michael Donaghy · *Conjure* · Picador Poetry · 2000

Tishani Doshi · *Countries of the Body: Contemporary World Poetry* · Aark Arts · 2006

Jane Draycott · *The Night Tree* · Carcanet · 2004

Carol Ann Duffy · *Mean Time* · Picador Poetry · 2013

Ian Duhig · *The Lammas Hireling* · Picador Poetry · 2012

Helen Dunmore · *Glad of These Times* · Bloodaxe Books · 2007

UA Fanthorpe · *Safe as Houses* · Peterloo Poets · 1995 · by permission of the Estate of UA Fanthorpe

Paul Farley · *Tramp in Flames* · Picador Poetry· 2012

Vicki Feaver · *The Handless Maiden* · Cape Poetry · 2009

Duncan Forbes · *Taking Liberties* · Enitharmon Press · 1993

Linda France · *The Simultaneous Dress* · Bloodaxe Books · 2002 · by permission of the author

Matthew Francis · *Dragons* · Faber & Faber · 2001

Pamela Gillilan · *The Rashomon Syndrome* · Bloodaxe Books · 1998 · by permission of the author

Alan Gillis · *Scapegoat* · 2014 · by kind permission of the author and The Gallery Press, Loughcrew, Oldcastle, County Meath, Ireland

John Goodby · *A True Prize* · Cinnamon Press · 2011 · by kind permission of the author

Lavinia Greenlaw · *A World Where News Travelled Slowly* · Faber & Faber · 2016

Thom Gunn · *The Man with Night Sweats* · Faber & Faber · 2002

Jen Hadfield · *Byssus* · Picador Poetry · 2014

Tony Harrison · *A Cold Coming* · Bloodaxe Books · 1991 · by permission of Faber & Faber

David Harsent · *Selected Poems: 1969-2005* · Faber & Faber · 2007

Seamus Heaney · *District and Circle* · Faber & Faber · 2011

Stuart Henson · *Ember Music* · Peterloo Poets · 1994 · by permission of the author

WN Herbert · *Cabaret McGonagall* · Bloodaxe Books · 1995

Geoffrey Hill · *The Orchards of Syon* · Counterpoint · 2002
Selima Hill · *Gloria: Selected Poems* · Bloodaxe Books · 2009
Ellen Hinsey · *Update on the Descent* · Bloodaxe Books · 2009
Sarah Howe · *Loop of Jade* · Chatto & Windus · 2015
Ted Hughes · *Birthday Letters* · Faber & Faber · 2002
Clive James · *Sentenced to Life* · Picador Poetry · 2015
Kathleen Jamie · *The Tree House* · Picador Poetry · 2004
Alan Jenkins · *A Shorter Life* · Chatto & Windus · 2005
Linton Kwesi Johnson · *Tings and Times* · Bloodaxe Books · 1991 ·
    by permission of LKJ Music Publishers
Jackie Kay · *Darling: New & Selected Poems* · Bloodaxe Books · 2007
Mimi Khalvati · *The Weather Wheel* · Carcanet · 2014
John Kinsella · *The Hierarchy of Sheep* · Bloodaxe Books · 2000 ·
    Fremantle · 2001 · reproduced courtesy of the author
August Kleinzahler · *The Hotel Oneira* · Faber & Faber · 2013
RF Langley · *Complete Poems*, ed. Jeremy Noel-Tod · Carcanet · 2015
James Lasdun · *Water Sessions* · Cape Poetry · 2012
Gwyneth Lewis · *Chaotic Angels: Poems in English* · Bloodaxe Books · 2005
Michael Longley · *A Hundred Doors* · Cape Poetry · 2011
Hannah Lowe · *Chick* · Bloodaxe Books · 2013
Roddy Lumsden · *Mischief Night: New & Selected Poems* · Bloodaxe Books · 2004
Derek Mahon · *The Yellow Book* · 1997 · by kind permission of the author
    and The Gallery Press, Loughcrew, Oldcastle, County Meath, Ireland
Glyn Maxwell · *Pluto* · Picador Poetry · 2013
Roger McGough · *The Way Things Are* · Penguin Books Ltd · 2000
Jamie McKendrick · *The Kiosk on the Brink* · Oxford Paperbacks · 1993
Kei Miller · *The Cartographer Tries to Map a Way to Zion* · Carcanet · 2014
Sinéad Morrissey · *Parallax* · Carcanet · Farrar, Straus & Giroux · 2013
Paul Muldoon · *Hay* · Faber & Faber · 2010
Les Murray · *Subhuman Redneck Poems* · Carcanet · Farrar, Straus &
    Giroux · 1996 · by permission of the publishers and the Margaret
    Connolly Agency
Daljit Nagra · *Look We Have Coming to Dover!* · Faber & Faber · 2005
Sean O'Brien · *The Drowned Book* · Picador Poetry · 2015
Alice Oswald · *The Thing in the Gap-Stone Stile* · Faber & Faber · 2007 ·
    by permission of the publishers and United Agents LLP on behalf of
    Alice Oswald

Don Paterson · *Nil Nil* · Faber & Faber · 2010

Clare Pollard · *Bedtime* · Bloodaxe Books · 2002

Peter Porter · *Max is Missing* · Picador Poetry· 2001

Sheenagh Pugh · *Stonelight* · Seren · 1999

Claudia Rankine · *Citizen: An American Lyric* · Penguin Books Ltd · 2015

Denise Riley · *Say Something Back* · Picador Poetry · 2016

Michael Symmons Roberts · *Burning Babylon* · Cape Poetry · 2001

Robin Robertson · *The Wrecking Light* · Picador Poetry · 2010 · by
permission of the author

Ann Sansom · *Romance* · Bloodaxe Books · 1994

Carole Satyamurti · *Stitching the Dark: New & Selected Poems* ·
Bloodaxe Books · 2005

Jo Shapcott · *Her Book: Poems 1988-1998* · Faber & Faber · 2006

Owen Sheers · *The Blue Book* · Seren · 2000

Penelope Shuttle · *Unsent: New & Selected Poems, 1980-2012* · Bloodaxe
Books · 2012 · by permission of David Higham Associates

George Szirtes · *New & Collected Poems* · Bloodaxe Books · 2008

Kate Tempest · *Hold Your Own* · Picador Poetry · 2014

RS Thomas · *Collected Later Poems: 1988-2000* · Bloodaxe Books · 2004

Derek Walcott · *White Egrets* · Faber & Faber · 2011

Lucy Anne Watt · unpublished · winner of Torbay Open Poetry
Competition

Hugo Williams · *Dock Leaves* · Faber & Faber · 1994

Benjamin Zephaniah · *City Psalms* · Bloodaxe Books · 1992

Winners of the Forward Prizes

Best Collection

2015 · Claudia Rankine · *Citizen: An American Lyric* · Penguin Books

2014 · Kei Miller · *The Cartographer Tries to Map a Way to Zion* · Carcanet

2013 · Michael Symmons Roberts · *Drysalter* · Cape Poetry

2012 · Jorie Graham · *PLACE* · Carcanet

2011 · John Burnside · *Black Cat Bone* · Cape Poetry

2010 · Seamus Heaney · *Human Chain* · Faber & Faber

2009 · Don Paterson · *Rain* · Faber & Faber

2008 · Mick Imlah · *The Lost Leader* · Faber & Faber

2007 · Sean O'Brien · *The Drowned Book* · Picador Poetry

2006 · Robin Robertson · *Swithering* · Picador Poetry

2005 · David Harsent · *Legion* · Faber & Faber

2004 · Kathleen Jamie · *The Tree House* · Picador Poetry

2003 · Ciaran Carson · *Breaking News* · The Gallery Press

2002 · Peter Porter · *Max is Missing* · Picador Poetry

2001 · Sean O'Brien · *Downriver* · Picador Poetry

2000 · Michael Donaghy · *Conjure* · Picador Poetry

1999 · Jo Shapcott · *My Life Asleep* · OUP

1998 · Ted Hughes · *Birthday Letters* · Faber & Faber

1997 · Jamie McKendrick · *The Marble Fly* · OUP

1996 · John Fuller · *Stones and Fires* · Chatto & Windus

1995 · Sean O'Brien · *Ghost Train* · OUP

1994 · Alan Jenkins · *Harm* · Chatto & Windus

1993 · Carol Ann Duffy · *Mean Time* · Anvil Press

1992 · Thom Gunn · *The Man with Night Sweats* · Faber & Faber

Best First Collection

2015 · Mona Arshi · *Small Hands* · Liverpool University Press

2014 · Liz Berry · *Black Country* · Chatto & Windus

2013 · Emily Berry · *Dear Boy* · Faber & Faber

2012 · Sam Riviere · *81 Austerities* · Faber & Faber

2011 · Rachael Boast · *Sidereal* · Picador Poetry

2010 · Hilary Menos · *Berg* · Seren

2009 · Emma Jones · *The Striped World* · Faber & Faber

2008 · Kathryn Simmonds · *Sunday at the Skin Launderette* · Seren
2007 · Daljit Nagra · *Look We Have Coming to Dover!* · Faber & Faber
2006 · Tishani Doshi · *Countries of the Body* · Aark Arts
2005 · Helen Farish · *Intimates* · Cape Poetry
2004 · Leontia Flynn · *These Days* · Cape Poetry
2003 · AB Jackson · *Fire Stations* · Anvil Press
2002 · Tom French · *Touching the Bones* · The Gallery Press
2001 · John Stammers · *Panoramic Lounge-Bar* · Picador Poetry
2000 · Andrew Waterhouse · *In* · The Rialto
1999 · Nick Drake · *The Man in the White Suit* · Bloodaxe Books
1998 · Paul Farley · *The Boy from the Chemist is Here to See You* ·
Picador Poetry
1997 · Robin Robertson · *A Painted Field* · Picador Poetry
1996 · Kate Clanchy · *Slattern* · Chatto & Windus
1995 · Jane Duran · *Breathe Now, Breathe* · Enitharmon
1994 · Kwame Dawes · *Progeny of Air* · Peepal Tree
1993 · Don Paterson · *Nil Nil* · Faber & Faber
1992 · Simon Armitage · *Kid* · Faber & Faber

Best Single Poem
2015 · Claire Harman · The Mighty Hudson · *Times Literary Supplement*
2014 · Stephen Santus · In a Restaurant · Bridport Prize
2013 · Nick MacKinnon · The Metric System · *The Warwick Review*
2012 · Denise Riley · A Part Song · *London Review of Books*
2011 · RF Langley · To a Nightingale · *London Review of Books*
2010 · Julia Copus · An Easy Passage · *Magma*
2009 · Robin Robertson · At Roane Head · *London Review of Books*
2008 · Don Paterson · Love Poem for Natalie "Tusja" Beridze ·
The Poetry Review
2007 · Alice Oswald · Dunt · *Poetry London*
2006 · Sean O'Brien · Fantasia on a Theme of James Wright ·
The Poetry Review
2005 · Paul Farley · Liverpool Disappears for a Billionth of a Second ·
The North
2004 · Daljit Nagra · Look We Have Coming to Dover! · *The Poetry Review*
2003 · Robert Minhinnick · The Fox in the Museum of Wales ·
Poetry London

2002 · Medbh McGuckian · She Is in the Past, She Has This Grace ·
   The Shop
2001 · Ian Duhig · The Lammas Hireling · National Poetry Competition
2000 · Tessa Biddington · The Death of Descartes · Bridport Prize
1999 · Robert Minhinnick · Twenty-five Laments for Iraq · *PN Review*
1998 · Sheenagh Pugh · Envying Owen Beattie · *New Welsh Review*
1997 · Lavinia Greenlaw · A World Where News Travelled Slowly ·
   Times Literary Supplement
1996 · Kathleen Jamie · The Graduates · *Times Literary Supplement*
1995 · Jenny Joseph · In Honour of Love · *The Rialto*
1994 · Iain Crichton Smith · Autumn · *PN Review*
1993 · Vicki Feaver · Judith · *Independent on Sunday*
1992 · Jackie Kay · Black Bottom · Bloodaxe Books

For more detail and further reading about the Forward Prizes, books and associated programmes, see our website forwardartsfoundation.org or follow us on Facebook or Twitter @forwardprizes